THE UNOFFICIAL HOGWARTS FOR THE HOLIDAYS COOKBOOK

75 RECIPES FOR A YEAR OF MAGICAL CELEBRATIONS

RITA MOCK-PIKE

ULYSSES PRESS

Published by:
ULYSSES PRESS
P.O. Box 3440
Berkeley, CA 94703
www.ulyssespress.com

ISBN: 978-1-64604-072-8
Library of Congress Control Number: 2020935669

Printed in China
10 9 8 7 6

Acquisitions editor: Claire Sielaff
Managing editor: Claire Chun
Editor: Renee Rutledge
Proofreader: Kathy Kaiser
Front cover and interior design: David Hastings
Artwork: shutterstock.com

IMPORTANT NOTE TO READERS: This book is an independent and unauthorized fan publication. No endorsement or sponsorship by or affiliation with J. K. Rowling, her publishers, or other copyright or trademark holders is claimed or suggested. All references in this book to copyrighted or trademarked characters or other elements of the J. K. Rowling books are for the purpose of commentary, criticism, analysis, or literary discussion only. The works of J. K. Rowling referenced in this book are publications of Scholastic Books (US), Raincoast Books (Canada), and Bloomsbury Publishing (UK), and readers are encouraged to buy and read these books.

To magically minded fans around the world

Contents

Introduction

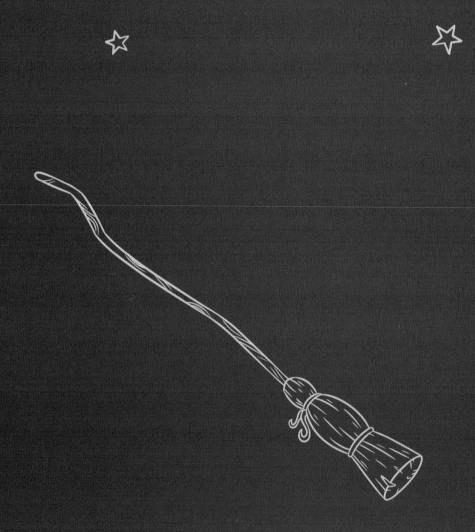

Whether you've grown up with these books or have just started reading them for the first time, something about the magic of Hogwarts has captured your heart, as it has millions of fans worldwide. No matter if you're a cunning serpent, a courageous lion, a wise eagle, or a loyal badger, it's true for everyone that coming back to these stories feels like coming home.

Throughout these adventures, our favorite characters faced struggles, heartbreak, danger, and many magical mishaps. It's the moments when they matured as people, grew together as friends, and learned much more than just witchcraft and wizardry that we hold close to our hearts and look back upon fondly when we recall those beloved pages.

So where does cooking come in? Since some of the most iconic moments happened around meal-times and holidays at the castle, it makes sense to reconnect with your favorite wizarding world by re-creating the dishes from those moments in your own kitchen.

This cookbook is organized by season, and then by holiday feast. It will cover all of the most important holidays celebrated at the castle (and over the summer break), from pumpkin treats in the fall to heart-shaped sweets in the spring. And in accordance with Hogwarts tradition, these feasts will feature largely English fare, comfort-food staples, and, of course, decadent desserts. For the fussier dishes, you'll find that the recipes have been pared down to make the final product easier to achieve if you don't have the help of a wand or self-stirring cauldron. That being said, the dishes you'll make with the help of this cookbook will certainly taste as fantastical as the ones from your favorite books. We hope you will come back to *The Unofficial Hogwarts for the Holidays Cookbook* for every season! Enjoy!

Fall Recipes

Nothing quite compares to the wonders of autumn: A chill in the air. Shorter days and longer nights. The smell of leaves and mist. A landscape painted in orange, red, and yellow. While for some non-magical folk this means mourning the loss of summer and dreading the start of another school year, young witches and wizards are eager for another year of classes at the castle. New adventures await. And though there will be homework, long lectures, and exams, new friends, new accomplishments, and, of course, feasts are also in store!

Snacks for a Train Ride

Watching the countryside roll by during a long train ride can make anyone hungry! As you settle into your seat and catch up with your friends aboard the scarlet steam engine, these are some tasty snacks and sweet treats to nibble on.

Corned Beef Sandwiches

Though our red-haired, hand-me-down-robe-wearing best friend doesn't particularly love corned beef sandwiches, they are actually perfect for lunch on the go. You'll find yourself going in for seconds of this filling, savory, and customizable treat.

Yield
4 sandwiches

Prep time
5 minutes

Cook time
5 minutes

Dressing
½ cup olive oil mayonnaise
1 tablespoon dill pickle juice
1 teaspoon dill pickle relish
1 teaspoon lemon juice
1 teaspoon horseradish sauce

Sandwiches
3 to 4 tablespoons
softened butter
8 slices rye bread
8 slices Swiss cheese
1 pound thinly sliced
cooked corned beef
1 cup sauerkraut, drained

1. Preheat a cast-iron skillet over medium heat.
2. To make the dressing, blend all of the ingredients together in a small mixing bowl. Set aside.
3. Butter one side of each slice of bread.
4. Place the buttered side of the bread down in the skillet.
5. Immediately place 1 piece of Swiss cheese on each slice of bread in the pan.
6. Add approximately ¼ pound of corned beef on each slice of bread.
7. Spoon out ¼ cup of sauerkraut over each slice, then top with about ¼ of the dressing.
8. Cap off the sandwich with another slice of bread, buttered-side up.
9. Flip the sandwich and let brown for another 1 to 2 minutes, until both sides are golden brown.
10. Remove from the heat and serve immediately.

NOTES
- The best way to flip the sandwiches is with a pair of tongs or with 2 wooden spatulas or spoons.
- Squeeze the bread and fillers together as you flip to prevent losing the goodies inside.
- If for some reason you need to swap out the corned beef, you can use Genoa salami and still have nearly the same flavor.

Pumpkin Pasties

A magical must-have, pumpkin pasties are an autumnal tradition. Warm, packed with pumpkin flavor, and immensely satisfying, these iconic treats are sure to be a crowd-pleaser. Plus, thanks to the fact that they're encased in a delicious golden crust, they are super portable. Perfect for a train ride!

Yield
6 pasties

Prep time
15 minutes

Cook time
30 minutes

Set time
1 hour

Filling
1 cup canned pumpkin puree
1 green apple, minced
¼ cup granulated sugar
pinch of ground nutmeg
pinch of ground cinnamon

Pastry Crust
1¼ cups all-purpose flour
1 tablespoon granulated sugar
¼ teaspoon salt
5 tablespoons cold butter, cut into chunks
3 tablespoons vegetable shortening, chilled and cut into chunks
4 to 6 tablespoons ice water

1. Combine all filling ingredients in a mixing bowl, mixing well until everything is thoroughly incorporated.
2. To make the crust, put the flour, sugar, and salt into a food processor bowl. Pulse several times to combine.
3. Scatter the chunks of butter and shortening over the flour mixture and pulse about 15 times until everything is combined and resembles a coarse meal. No powdery bits should remain.
4. Transfer the mixture to a large mixing bowl.
5. Sprinkle 4 tablespoons of ice water over the mixture, and toss it with a spatula until it starts to clump together. If the mixture is too dry, add 1 tablespoon of water at a time, until the texture is smooth.
6. Gather all the dough into a ball and pat it down into a disc.
7. Wrap the disc in plastic wrap and chill in the refrigerator for 1 hour.
8. After the dough has chilled, preheat the oven to 400°F.
9. Roll the dough to ⅛-inch thickness.
10. Use a saucer, small plate, or bowl to cut out 6-inch circles.
11. Put 1 to 2 teaspoons of filling into each circle, and fold the dough over into half circles.
12. Moisten the edges of each circle with ice water and crimp with a fork to seal.
13. Cut small slits into each pasty to make vents.
14. Bake the pasties on an ungreased cookie sheet for 30 minutes, or until browned.

Cauldron Cakes

Here's a fun take on the cauldron cake: a decadent chocolate cupcake topped with fiery orange frosting. These are so easy to make, anyone could do it!

Yield
12 cauldron cakes

Prep time
30 minutes

Cook time
12 to 15 minutes

Cool time
45 to 60 minutes

Cupcakes
1 cup all-purpose flour
¼ cup + 2 tablespoons cocoa powder
¼ teaspoon baking powder
¼ teaspoon baking soda
½ teaspoon salt
¼ cup olive oil
1 cup cane sugar
1 egg
½ teaspoon vanilla
½ cup milk, divided

Filling
¼ cup milk
2¼ teaspoons all-purpose flour
2½ teaspoons powdered hot chocolate mix
¼ cup butter, softened
¼ cup cane sugar
¼ teaspoon vanilla extract

1. Preheat the oven to 350°F. Grease or line a muffin tin and set aside.
2. Combine the flour, cocoa powder, baking soda, baking powder, and salt in a medium bowl.
3. In a separate bowl, mix together the oil and sugar until thoroughly combined.
4. Add the egg and vanilla to the oil mixture, and beat until fully incorporated.
5. Add in one third of the flour mixture and mix well. Add half of the milk and mix again.
6. Add another one third of the flour and mix well. Add the second half of the milk and combine thoroughly.
7. Finally, add the last of the flour mixture and mix until completely incorporated.
8. Spoon the batter into the muffin tins, filling them about halfway. Bake for 12 to 15 minutes or until a toothpick inserted into the center comes out clean.
9. Remove the cupcakes from the oven, then, with a knife, remove each cupcake from the tin to a cooling rack. Let cool completely, 45 to 60 minutes.
10. While the cupcakes cool, combine all the ingredients for the filling in a small saucepan over medium heat. Stir well until the mixture thickens, about 7 minutes, then remove it from the heat and cool completely.
11. Using an electric handheld mixer, mix the filling again for 5 minutes or until it becomes fluffy and light.
12. Once the filling is fluffed, use your thumb or a small spoon to press a hole in the cupcakes, creating a "cup" inside each one.
13. Fill each cup with the filling and let stand while you make the icing.

Icing
1 cup unsalted butter, softened
4½ cups powdered sugar
1 tablespoon vanilla extract
4 to 5 tablespoons heavy
cream or whole milk

14. To make the icing, beat the butter on medium speed with an electric handheld mixer until it is soft and creamy. While beating, gradually add in the powdered sugar, stopping the mixer every now and then to scrape down the sides with a spatula.

15. Once the sugar and butter are thoroughly incorporated, add the vanilla and beat again.

16. Add the heavy cream or milk 1 tablespoon at a time until the desired consistency is reached.

17. Let stand for 5 minutes, then frost your cauldron cakes and serve.

Licorice Wands

Now you can open your own wand shop, thanks to this easy and tasty recipe for licorice wands. Whether you fill your wands with phoenix tail feathers, unicorn hair, or dragon heartstrings—well—that's entirely up to you!

Yield
24 wands

Prep time
5 minutes

Cook time
2 to 3 minutes

Cool time
1 hour

6 ounces candy melts
or almond bark
24 licorice twists, any flavor
candy sprinkles, sugared dots,
or other small decorative pieces

1. Place the candy melts or almond bark in a glass measuring cup or bowl and microwave for 30 seconds. Stir.
2. Repeat until the candy is melted and smooth.
3. Dip one end of a licorice twist into the melted candy.
4. Place the candy sprinkles in a separate bowl.
5. Dip the licorice twist into the candy sprinkles and roll around, covering the candy coating with as many sprinkles as desired.
6. Repeat steps 3 and 5 with the remaining licorice twists.
7. Cool the twists on a waxed paper sheet for 1 hour or until the coating is firm.

Pepper Imp Bark

A delicious take on a classic wizarding treat, this peppermint bark recipe won't have you breathing fire or blowing smoke out of your nose but still packs a minty punch!

Yield
16 servings

Prep time
5 minutes

Cook time
20 minutes

Chill time
40 minutes

12 ounces semisweet
chocolate chips
1 cup dark chocolate chips
12 ounces white chocolate chips
½ teaspoon peppermint extract
8 candy canes, crushed

1. Line a rimmed baking sheet with parchment paper.
2. Place the semisweet and dark chocolate chips in a large microwavable bowl. Microwave on high for 30 seconds, then stir the chocolate with a metal spoon. Repeat microwaving for 30-second intervals until the chocolate is fully melted, about 10 minutes.
3. Pour the melted chocolate onto the baking sheet, and spread it evenly throughout the pan. Place the pan in the fridge and cool for 20 minutes.
4. Microwave the white chocolate chips on high in 30-second increments, about 10 minutes, until they have melted and can be poured over the chocolate layer.
5. Top immediately with crushed candy cane pieces.
6. Return the bark to the refrigerator for 20 minutes to finish setting.

Chocolate Balls Full of Clotted Cream and Strawberry Mousse

The train trolley offers a plethora of delectable sweets, but perhaps the most decadent are the stuffed chocolate balls. This recipe uses tangy strawberry mousse and clotted cream, resulting in a rich, bewitchingly delicious treat.

Yield
24 to 30 chocolate balls

Prep time
25 minutes

Chill time
40 minutes to 1 hour, 20 minutes

24 ounces almond bark or melting chocolate, divided
Clotted Cream (page 24)
Strawberry Mousse (page 25)
candy truffle mold

1. Melt half the chocolate according to package instructions.
2. Place the melted chocolate into a pastry bag, and squeeze a bit into each cavity of a truffle mold.
3. Using clean hands, tamp down the chocolate onto all the walls of the mold.
4. Let the chocolate set, 20 to 40 minutes. The chocolate will set much more quickly (about 20 minutes) in the refrigerator.
5. Once the chocolate has set, spoon ½ to 1 teaspoon of each of the Clotted Cream and Strawberry Mousse into the chocolate shells, either alternating between flavors or combining them in each shell.
6. Melt the remaining chocolate and put in the pastry bag. Squeeze out more chocolate over the tops of the Clotted Cream and the Strawberry Mousse.
7. Encapsulate the chocolate balls, tamping down the chocolate to seal.
8. Refrigerate for 20 to 40 minutes to set. The colder the chocolate, the easier it will be to remove the balls from the mold.
9. Carefully pop the chocolate balls out of the molds. It may take a few attempts to get them out without damaging them.

Clotted Cream

Cook time

12 hours

Chill time

8 hours to overnight

2 cups heavy cream
(not ultra-pasteurized)

Day 1

1. Preheat the oven to 175°F.
2. Pour the cream into a shallow casserole dish that allows it to spread out thinly.
3. Place the cream in the oven and cook for 12 hours, uncovered.
4. Check the cream at 8 hours and 10 hours if you're not totally sure that your oven is accurate with temperature. You only want the cream to develop a light tan color and not a darker brown shade.

Day 2

1. Remove the dish from the oven and let it cool to room temperature. There will be a skin on the cream—leave this alone.
2. Once the cream has cooled to room temperature, place it in the refrigerator and chill for 8 hours or overnight.

Day 3

1. Take the cream out of the refrigerator and gently remove the thick layer of clotted cream from the surface, leaving behind a thin liquid layer. Place in a bowl.
2. Gently stir the skimmed cream layer to create a smooth texture.
3. Stir the thin liquid into the clotted cream to reach the desired texture.
4. Store in the refrigerator until you're ready to use.

NOTES
The 12-hour cooking period for the clotted cream is easiest done overnight, unless your oven has an automatic safety shut-off feature. If your oven has a safety shut-off feature, you should do the baking stage during the day when you're at home to ensure you can keep the oven going.

Strawberry Mousse

Prep time
20 minutes

Chill time
20 minutes

2 cups hulled fresh strawberries
1 tablespoon cane sugar
½ pint heavy cream
3 egg whites

1. Add the strawberries to a food processor and chop to a large "meal" texture, leaving a few chunks. Transfer the strawberries to a mixing bowl.
2. Add the sugar to the bowl and mix.
3. In a separate bowl, whip the heavy cream with an electric handheld mixer until stiff peaks form. Fold the whipped cream into the strawberries and mix well.
4. In a separate bowl, beat the egg whites with clean beaters until stiff peaks form. Fold the egg whites into the strawberry mixture, again mixing well.
5. Chill the Strawberry Mousse in the refrigerator until you're ready to make the chocolate balls.

Nougat

A staple of any candy store, magical or not, nougat is a favorite. If you can't use an enchanted charm to monitor your cooking sugar's temperature, be sure to have a candy thermometer on hand. This recipe is a bit like fudge—follow the directions precisely or the nougat might not set and instead become a blob of sweet goo that re-forms in the pan every time you take out a square.

Yield
24 to 30 servings

Prep time
20 minutes

Cook time
45 to 50 minutes

Chill time
3 to 4 hours

Stage One
butter
3 large egg whites
1½ cups cane sugar
1¼ cups light corn syrup
¼ cup water

Stage Two
3 cups cane sugar
2⅔ cups light corn syrup
⅓ cup light honey

Stage Three
½ cup unsalted butter, melted
4 teaspoons vanilla extract
3 cups mixed nuts, such
as almonds, pecans,
walnuts, and pistachios
1 teaspoon salt

Stage One

1. Heavily butter a large mixing bowl and set aside.
2. With an electric handheld mixer or stand mixer, beat the egg whites until stiff peaks form, about 7 minutes.
3. In a saucepan over medium heat, combine the sugar, corn syrup, and water. Stir constantly until the sugar dissolves and the mixture comes to a boil, 6 to 7 minutes.
4. Once the sugar is dissolved, without stirring, cook the sugar mixture until the candy thermometer reads 260°F.
5. Carefully remove the pan from the heat and pour the mixture over the egg whites, with the mixer on low. Beat together until the mixture is able to hold its shape and is lukewarm, about 10 minutes.
6. Transfer the mixture to the buttered bowl.

Stage Two

1. In a large saucepan, combine the sugar, corn syrup, and honey over medium heat. Stir constantly with a clean spoon until the sugar dissolves and the mixture comes to a boil. Keep stirring the mixture over medium-high heat until the candy thermometer reads 275°F. This will take about 10 minutes.
2. Test the mixture by putting a partial spoonful into cold (or ice) water. If it comes together in a hard ball, it's ready. If not, you should cook the mixture a little bit longer until it does.

<u>Stage Three</u>

1. Heavily butter a 15 x 10-inch pan and set aside.
2. Pour the Stage Two mixture over the Stage One mixture in the buttered bowl.
3. Use a wooden spoon to stir the two mixtures together until they are thoroughly combined, about 3 minutes.
4. In a separate bowl, combine the butter and vanilla.
5. Pour the butter mixture into the other mixture and blend.
6. Add the nuts and salt to the mixture and stir together until well blended. Pour the whole thing into the prepared pan.
7. Let set for 3 to 4 hours or until firm. (Do not refrigerate.)
8. Cut into squares and wrap with waxed paper or plastic wrap, if desired.

Ice Cream (Sandwiches)

It's true—the trolley even offers ice cream! And while it might be asking too much of non-magical folk to bring frozen treats on a train, these ice cream sandwiches are portable (at least for a short period of time).

<u>Yield</u>
12 ice cream sandwiches

<u>Prep time</u>
20 minutes

<u>Bake time</u>
8 to 10 minutes

<u>Freeze time</u>
4 to 6 hours

3 cups all-purpose flour
1 teaspoon baking soda
1 teaspoon salt
½ teaspoon baking powder
1 cup unsalted butter, softened
1 cup cane sugar
1 cup packed brown sugar
2 large eggs
2 teaspoons vanilla extract
2 cups semisweet chocolate chips
6 cups ice cream
1 to 2 cups semisweet chocolate mini-chips (optional)

1. Preheat the oven to 375°F.
2. Line 2 baking sheets with parchment paper and set aside.
3. In a medium mixing bowl, combine the flour, baking soda, salt, and baking powder. Set aside.
4. In a separate bowl, thoroughly combine the butter and sugars until creamy.
5. Beat the eggs and vanilla into the butter mixture until it becomes fluffy and light.
6. Mix in the dry ingredients until completely combined.
7. Add in the chocolate chips, stirring them in with a wooden spoon.
8. As evenly as possible, divide the dough into 24 balls and place them on the cookie sheets. You don't want to make them too small or they won't hold enough ice cream. Nor do you want them too large—they will become brittle and hard to work with.
9. Bake in the oven for 8 to 10 minutes or until they have just barely started to turn golden brown.
10. Remove the cookies from the oven, and let them sit on the baking sheets for 2 minutes before removing them to a cooling rack or baking cloths.
11. Once the cookies have completely cooled, flip half the cookies over so that the flat, browned side is up. These will be your "bottoms" for the sandwiches.
12. Remove the ice cream from the freezer and let it stand for 2 minutes to soften slightly. Do not let it stand for too long or the ice cream will melt off the cookies in the freezer.
13. With a sturdy spoon or ice cream scoop, scoop out ½ cup of ice cream per sandwich and gently "smoosh" it onto the cookie bottom. If needed, use a butter knife to spread the ice cream across the cookies.

14. Top each sandwich with the second cookie and, if desired, press chocolate mini-chips into the ice cream on the sides of the sandwich.

15. Wrap each sandwich in parchment paper, and then wrap in foil and place in a freezer-proof container. Freeze for 4 to 6 hours before serving.

NOTES
Several flavors pair well with the chocolate chip cookies. Vanilla in all forms, salted caramel, chocolate, fudge swirl, and peanut butter all go famously in the sandwiches.

Pumpkin Tarts

This pumpkin tart is a delightful fall treat. Filled to the brim with cinnamon and pumpkin goodness, these tarts are sure to bewitch your taste buds.

Yield
16 tarts

Prep time
10 to 12 minutes

Cook time
25 to 28 minutes

Total time
35 to 40 minutes

Topping
¼ cup all-purpose flour
¼ cup cane sugar
2 tablespoons butter
1 teaspoon ground cinnamon
whipped cream, to serve

Crust
6 ounces cold cream cheese
¾ cup cold butter (12 tablespoons)
1½ cups all-purpose flour

Filling
1 (14-ounce) can sweetened condensed milk
1¼ cups cooked, mashed pumpkin
1 large egg
1½ teaspoons pumpkin pie spice

1. Preheat the oven to 375°F.
2. To make the topping, combine all of the ingredients except for the whipped cream in a small bowl. Using a fork, blend them completely until crumbly. Set aside.
3. To make the crust, combine the cream cheese and butter in a mixing bowl. Beat at medium speed until thoroughly incorporated.
4. Add in the flour and continue beating until the dough forms.
5. Divide the dough into 16 pieces and place the pieces in ungreased muffin pan sections. Press the dough in each section, forming the bottom and sides of the crust against the pan. It should be sufficiently thick on all sides.
6. Now, take all the filling ingredients and combine them in a bowl. Whisk them together until smooth.
7. Pour the filling into the crust "cups" in the muffin tins.
8. Sprinkle the topping onto each of the tarts.
9. Place the muffin tin(s) in the oven and bake the tarts for 25 to 28 minutes or until the crusts turn golden brown and the filling has solidified.
10. Cool the tarts in the pan(s) for 5 minutes, then run a sharp knife around the inside edge of the cups to loosen the tarts.
11. Remove the tarts to a cooling rack and let cool until they reach room temperature.
12. Garnish the tarts with a dollop of whipped cream and serve.

NOTES
Any leftover tarts should be stored in the refrigerator after they have cooled. If you need a gluten-free alternative, simply use a 1-to-1 flour option instead of wheat all-purpose flour. This 1-to-1 option should include xanthan gum in the mixture.

Chocolate Frogs

This recipe is surprisingly easy and is sure to delight any Potterhead. The only specialty utensil is a frog-shaped mold, available online. Feel free to enchant your frogs after you're done making them, but be careful! Don't let them escape out the train window.

Yield
24 to 36 frogs, depending on mold size

Prep time
10 minutes

Cook time
10 to 13 minutes

Set time
4 hours

12 ounces semisweet chocolate chips
2 tablespoons unsalted butter
4 tablespoons milk
miniature marshmallows, pecan halves in pieces, or shredded coconut (optional)

1. Lightly spray a candy mold with coconut oil cooking spray.
2. Combine the chocolate and butter in a double boiler over medium heat, stirring constantly until the chocolate begins to melt, 5 minutes.
3. Once the chocolate is quickly melting, reduce the heat to low. Continue stirring for 2 to 3 minutes.
4. Add the milk, 1 tablespoon at a time, until it is thoroughly combined and the chocolate is smooth and easy to pour, 3 to 5 minutes.
5. Remove the mixture from the heat and immediately start spooning the chocolate into the molds. Be sure to push the chocolate into any crevices of the mold. If you wish to add filling, fill the molds only halfway.
6. Add miniature marshmallows, pecans, coconut, or other filling choices, if using, to the middle of the chocolate mold, then top the rest of the mold with chocolate. Smooth the back off with a butter knife.
7. Place the mold in the refrigerator and chill for at least 4 hours before serving.

Start-of-Term Feast

As you take your place at a long table under the warm light of floating candles, you can smell the enticing scent of good things cooking. Roast beef, gravy, potatoes, and more—it's all waiting for you at the first feast of the year. And after the enchanted hat has finished its song and its sorting of the first-years, it's time to tuck in!

Roast Beef

Meat Choices

Roast beef is a classic dish for any special occasion. But don't be intimidated. Even if you're a beginner in the kitchen, you don't need the skills of a house elf to make truly tasty roast beef. And be sure to save those leftovers—they make a perfect next-day sandwich.

Yield
6 to 7 servings

Prep time
2 hours, 20 minutes

Cook time
3 hours, plus 30 minutes to rest

3 to 3½ pounds round roast
3 or 4 cloves garlic, slivered
olive oil
salt
ground pepper
dried rosemary
dried thyme
dried parsley

1. Let the round roast sit at room temperature for 2 hours to help it cook evenly.
2. Once the meat has evenly warmed, preheat the oven to 365°F.
3. Remove the wrapping from the meat and thoroughly rinse.
4. Pat the roast dry with paper towels and set on a plate.
5. Using a knife, slit several holes around the roast. Place slivers of garlic into each incision.
6. Brush olive oil over the whole roast.
7. Sprinkle the salt, pepper, rosemary, thyme, and parsley over the roast.
8. Position a rimmed baking sheet or pan under the lower rack of your oven. The pan will catch the drippings from the roast.
9. Place the roast directly on the lower rack, fat-side up, over the pan.
10. Roast for 3 hours.
11. When the internal temperature is between 135°F and 140°F, the roast is ready. Remove it from the oven and place it on a cutting board.
12. Tent foil over the meat and let it rest for 30 minutes before carving. This helps to seal in the juices.
13. Thinly slice the meat and serve.

Fancy Pork Chops

This pork chop recipe takes the humble chop to the next level and makes it worthy of one of the most magical feasts of the year. And whether you're a prefect in the kitchen or more of a first-year, this recipe will help you get the most spellbindingly tasty results.

Yield
4 to 6 servings

Prep time
1 hour, 15 minutes

Cook time
35 to 45 minutes

4 to 6 pork chops

Brine
6 cups warm water
¾ cup cane sugar
2 tablespoons salt

Topping
1 tablespoon olive oil
1 onion, finely chopped
1 tablespoon cane sugar
juice of 2 oranges
⅓ cup dried cranberries
⅓ cup chopped dried apricots
2 tablespoons apple cider vinegar
⅓ cup chopped pecans
¼ teaspoon sea salt
½ teaspoon dried thyme (optional)
½ teaspoon dried rosemary (optional)

1. To make the brine, place the warm water, sugar, and salt in a container large enough to lay out the chops without stacking them. Stir together until the sugar and salt have mostly dissolved.
2. Lay the pork chops in the brine, and spoon the brine over the chops until all of the meat is coated.
3. Cover the container and place in the refrigerator for 1 hour.
4. While the meat is marinating, make the topping by heating the olive oil in a cast-iron skillet until it simmers.
5. Add the onion and sugar. Stir together until the onion is browned thoroughly.
6. Turn the temperature to low and let the onion mixture simmer.
7. Add the orange juice, cranberries, and apricots to a medium saucepan over medium heat and bring to a simmer.
8. Once the mixture is simmering, add in the onion mixture, including all the liquid, to the fruit mixture.
9. Next, add apple cider vinegar, pecans, and sea salt. Thoroughly combine.
10. Keep on low heat, simmering until the pork chops have marinated the full hour.
11. Preheat oven to 450°F. Place the oven rack on the lower-middle position and place a rimmed baking sheet on the rack.
12. Remove the fruit mixture from the heat.
13. Remove the pork chops from the brine. Rinse them well and dry them with a paper towel.
14. Reheat the cast-iron skillet in which you cooked the onions to medium-high.
15. Brown each chop for 3 to 4 minutes per side.

16. Once the chops are slightly browned, place them on the pan in the oven.
17. Top the chops with the topping mixture, portioning it out equally across all the chops. If using, sprinkle the thyme and rosemary over the chops.
18. Bake the chops for 15 minutes.
19. Using a meat thermometer, check the internal temperature of the pork chops. If they have reached 145°F, remove from the oven.
20. Let the chops stand for 5 minutes, then serve hot.

Bacon-Wrapped Sausage Bites

These are an easy yet extremely satisfying side dish or appetizer for any grand meal. The bacon adds a salty kick to the savory flavor of the cocktail sausages. Serve on a platter with a cup of toothpicks on the side for easy eating.

Yield
10 to 15 servings

Prep time
7 to 10 minutes

Cook time
30 to 40 minutes

brown sugar
1 pound thick-cut bacon, halved lengthwise
7 ounces cocktail sausages

1. Preheat the oven to 400°F.
2. Line a rimmed baking sheet with aluminum foil and sprinkle the foil lightly with brown sugar.
3. Wrap the narrow strips of bacon around the sausages and place them on the pan.
4. Sprinkle more brown sugar over the meat.
5. Bake for 30 to 40 minutes or until the bacon is crisp.

Yorkshire Pudding

Yorkshire pudding is a traditional English side dish that's been made since the 1700s! It's no wonder that witches and wizards also love it—Yorkshire pudding is as versatile as it is easy to make.

Yield
10 to 12 servings

Prep time
10 minutes

Cook time
30 to 40 minutes

½ cup beef suet, drippings, butter, or shortening
¾ cup all-purpose flour
½ teaspoon salt
3 eggs
¾ cup milk

1. Preheat the oven to 450°F.
2. Evenly divide the suet between each of the 12 muffin cups. Set aside.
3. Sift the flour and salt in a small bowl. Set aside.
4. In a medium mixing bowl, combine the eggs and milk and beat until light and foamy.
5. As soon as the oven is at temperature, place the pan with the suet on the middle rack. Heat until the fat is smoking hot, which should take 15 to 20 minutes.
6. With a wooden spoon, combine the dry mixture into the egg mixture until just incorporated. Be careful not to overmix.
7. Remove the pan from the oven once the fat is smoking hot and carefully pour the batter into the pan.
8. Return the pan to the oven and bake for 15 to 20 minutes or until the pudding is puffy and dry.
9. Remove the pan from the oven and let the pudding cool for 5 minutes before serving.
10. If there's a little oil remaining on the top of the pudding, drain it carefully before serving.

Mashed Potatoes

Every great feast needs some stellar side dishes, and mashed potatoes are arguably the king of all sides. This recipe is full of creamy, buttery goodness and is sure to please any witch, wizard, or nearly-headless ghost at the table.

Yield

6 servings

Prep time

15 minutes

Cook time

20 minutes

2 pounds russet potatoes, peeled and chopped into eighths

1 cup milk

2 tablespoons butter

½ teaspoon Italian seasoning

½ teaspoon parsley flakes

½ teaspoon salt

½ teaspoon freshly ground black pepper

½ teaspoon minced onion

½ teaspoon garlic powder

½ teaspoon dried cilantro

1. In a large saucepot, bring water with a pinch of salt to a boil.
2. Once the water is boiling, place the potatoes in the water and cook for 15 minutes, or until tender.
3. Carefully drain the potatoes and return them to the saucepot.
4. Add the milk and butter to a small saucepan over medium-low heat. Stir until the butter melts.
5. Bring the milk and butter mix to a boil, stirring occasionally to prevent burning.
6. While you are waiting for the milk and butter mix to boil, use a large fork or potato masher to mash the potatoes.
7. Once the butter and milk mix boils, remove it from the heat.
8. Gently stir the milk and butter mixture into the mashed potatoes, until the potatoes become creamy.
9. Work the potatoes with a large fork until they become fluffy.
10. Thoroughly blend in the spices.
11. Serve hot.

Gravy

A rich, thick gravy is key to any sumptuous feast. Feel free to sprinkle the spices you prefer into your cauldron—this is a potion that benefits from experimentation (unlike the one that will, with just one wrong ingredient, turn you into a cat-human hybrid).

Yield
12 to 14 servings

Prep time
2 to 5 minutes

Cook time
10 minutes

2 tablespoons unsalted butter
½ cup all-purpose flour, divided
2 cups beef, poultry,
or vegetable stock

1. In a medium saucepan, melt the butter over medium-high heat.
2. Once the butter has melted completely, whisk in half the flour. It will make a thick paste. Let it cook for 1 to 2 minutes.
3. Slowly pour in the stock and whisk well, stirring continuously for 5 minutes.
4. Whisk in the remainder of the flour and keep stirring until the gravy is thick and creamy.
5. Remove the gravy from the heat and let it stand for 2 to 3 minutes before serving.

Desserts

Spotted Dick

Spotted dick is named as such because of the dried fruit speckled throughout the pudding. In this instance, "dick" hearkens back to an old, colloquial term for pudding. Though the name of this dish might sound a bit rude at first, it actually just means "spotted pudding." This English classic is often served with creamy custard.

Yield
12 to 16 servings

Prep time
15 minutes

Cook time
2 hours

1 cup dried cherries
2 cups raisins
2 cups golden raisins
1½ cups dried cranberries
3¾ cups blanched
slivered almonds
1 cup shortening
1 cup cane sugar
5 large eggs
4 tablespoons vanilla extract
3 cups all-purpose flour
3 teaspoons baking powder
1 teaspoon salt
Custard Cream Sauce
(page 45)

1. Preheat the oven to 300°F.
2. Grease and flour a 10-inch tube pan.
3. Combine the dried fruit and nuts together in a bowl.
4. In a separate bowl, whisk the shortening and sugar until light and fluffy.
5. Beat the eggs and vanilla into the shortening mixture.
6. In another bowl, combine the flour, baking powder, and salt.
7. Combine the flour mixture with the shortening mixture. Mix well and pour over the fruit and nuts, stirring everything together until everything is coated.
8. Transfer the whole mixture into the prepared tube pan.
9. Bake for 2 hours or until a toothpick can be inserted into the center and come out clean.
10. Remove from the oven and cool for 10 minutes before removing from the pan to a cooling rack.
11. Let cool completely, then pour the Custard Cream Sauce on top and serve.

Custard Cream Sauce

Prep time
5 minutes

Cook time
10 minutes

1 cup fresh cream
1½ cups whole milk
½ cup cane sugar, divided
1 vanilla pod, split
lengthwise and scraped
(keep pod and beans)
6 egg yolks
ice bath

1. Add the cream, milk, ¼ cup of sugar, and vanilla pod and beans to a medium saucepan, and simmer over medium heat until the mixture starts to bubble at the edges. Let bubble for 2 minutes, but do not let it get to a boil.
2. Remove the cream mixture from the heat and let stand for 10 to 20 minutes, not completely cooling.
3. While the cream mixture is cooling, whisk together the egg yolks and remaining ¼ cup of sugar in a medium bowl.
4. Ladle some of the cream mixture into the egg yolk mixture and swiftly whisk together to combine.
5. Add more cream mixture and repeat until the egg mixture is warm.
6. Pour the warm egg mixture into the remaining cream mixture in the saucepan. Return the pan to the stove.
7. Continue cooking the mixture over medium heat while constantly stirring for 5 to 7 minutes, until the custard starts to coat the back of the spoon.
8. Once the custard has thickened, remove it from the heat and strain it through a sieve into a medium bowl. This will remove lumps and the vanilla pod and beans.
9. Place the custard in an ice bath to cool it down quickly and prevent overcooking.
10. Once the Custard Cream Sauce has cooled, serve with the Spotted Dick or cover and store for up to 4 days.

NOTES

When cutting the pudding, use a serrated knife to keep the slices smooth.

Rice Pudding

The foundation of this classic rice pudding is a simple mixture of rice and water or milk, but the toppings are where you can really spice things up. Try some colorful berries or fruits in colors that show your House pride, or load up on the chocolate for a more decadent take. You can never go wrong with rice pudding!

Yield
6 to 8 servings

Prep time
15 minutes

Cook time
10 to 12 minutes

2 cups cooked rice
½ cup milk
¼ cup cane sugar
¼ teaspoon salt
1 tablespoon cocoa powder
½ teaspoon vanilla extract
⅓ cup semisweet chocolate chips
whipped cream, for garnish
cinnamon, for garnish

1. Combine all of the ingredients except for the chocolate chips and garnishes in a medium saucepan over medium-low heat, stirring until fully blended.
2. Turn the heat to low and let simmer.
3. Melt the chocolate chips in the microwave for 30-second intervals until soft and creamy.
4. Add the chocolate chips to the saucepan and stir them in thoroughly with the other ingredients.
5. Simmer on low for 10 to 12 minutes, stirring every minute or two to avoid burning.
6. Remove the pan from the heat and let the Rice Pudding stand for 10 minutes before serving. (Or, if preferred, chill for 2 hours and serve.)
7. Garnish with a dollop of whipped cream and lightly sprinkle with cinnamon to serve.

Chocolate Gâteau

If you're looking for decadence that is absolutely transcendent, look no further. This dense, rich cake is separated by layers of creamy chocolate frosting and is the perfect grand finale of any successful feast.

Yield
10 servings

Prep time
40 minutes

Cook time
45 minutes

1 cup hot coffee
1¾ cups all-purpose flour
2 cups cane sugar
¾ cup unsweetened cocoa powder
2 teaspoons baking soda
1 teaspoon baking powder
½ teaspoon salt
1 cup buttermilk
½ cup applesauce
2 extra-large eggs
1 teaspoon vanilla extract
Chocolate Cream Filling (page 50)
Chocolate Frosting (page 50)
strawberries, pecans, or meringues, for garnish

1. Preheat the oven to 350°F.
2. Butter and flour two springform pans or 8-inch round cake pans. Set aside.
3. Brew 1 cup of strong coffee and set aside.
4. In a large mixing bowl, sift together the flour, sugar, cocoa powder, baking soda, baking powder, and salt.
5. Next, in a bottle or jar, combine the buttermilk, applesauce, eggs, and vanilla extract, stirring to completely incorporate the ingredients.
6. Slowly pour the buttermilk mixture into the bowl with the dry ingredients, and whisk them together with an electric handheld mixer on a low speed.
7. Add the hot coffee and stir with a spatula until everything is just combined. Do not overmix. Scrape down the sides of the bowl as you mix.
8. Divide the mixture into 2 equal parts and pour into the pans.
9. Bake for 40 to 45 minutes, or until a toothpick inserted into the middle of the cakes comes out mostly clean.
10. Let cool in the pan for 10 minutes, then transfer to wire racks to cool completely.
11. Once the cakes have completely cooled, use an electric handheld mixer to whisk the Chocolate Cream Filling until stiff peaks form.
12. Place one cake on a cake platter and spread one layer of cream filling on the first cake.
13. Lay the second cake over the first and frost the top and sides with the Chocolate Frosting.
14. Garnish with your choice of berries, nuts, or meringue pieces.

Chocolate Cream Filling

Prep time
8 to 10 minutes

Cook time
7 to 10 minutes

Chill time
overnight

2 cups double cream
3½ ounces high-quality
European milk chocolate,
finely chopped
3½ ounces high-quality
European dark chocolate,
70 to 75% cacao

Make the Chocolate Cream Filling 1 day before baking the cake.

1. Pour the double cream into a small saucepan and carefully bring to a boil, stirring enough to prevent burning.
2. Remove the pan from the heat and add the chocolate to the cream.
3. Slowly stir until the chocolate has melted into the cream.
4. Cover the filling and let cool completely before placing in the refrigerator overnight.

Chocolate Frosting

Prep time
5 to 6 minutes

Cook time
6 to 9 minutes

Cool time
30 minutes

6 tablespoons milk
3 tablespoons unsweetened
cocoa powder
½ cup butter
3¾ cups powdered sugar

1. Add the milk, cocoa, and butter to a medium saucepan over medium-low heat.
2. Bring to a boil, stirring occasionally to prevent burning.
3. Remove the pan from the heat once the mixture has reached the boiling point.
4. Pour the cocoa mixture into a mixing bowl.
5. Add the powdered sugar and blend with an electric handheld mixer to completely smooth out all lumps.
6. Stir occasionally to keep the mixture smooth while it cools completely.

Strawberry Trifle

Trifle can be a very magnificent dessert, especially when served in a clear glass dish so that your guests can see its many layers. This recipe uses strawberries, sponge cake, and cream to create beautiful, eye-catching layers. Be sure to summon a big group of friends and family (or perhaps a half-giant) to help you eat this gargantuan dessert!

Yield
20 servings

Prep time
15 to 20 minutes

4 cups vanilla pudding, divided
6 cups quartered fresh strawberries, divided
1 (9 x 13-inch) cake of choice (lemon cake highly recommended), cubed, divided
1 (8-ounce) tub whipped cream, divided

1. Place 2 cups of pudding in the bottom of a large trifle bowl, glass vase, glass mixing bowl, or glass salad bowl.
2. Add a layer of strawberries to the dish, positioning them carefully to keep them above the pudding layer.
3. Add a layer of cake cubes to the bowl.
4. Add another layer of pudding, topped with a light layer of whipped cream.
5. Add another layer of strawberries.
6. Repeat the layers of whipped cream, cake, and strawberries until the container is full.
7. Top with fresh berries.
8. Garnish with dollops of whipped cream.
9. Let the crowds admire, and then serve.

Treacle Tarts

Treacle tart isn't just another English staple, it's also our bespectacled, be-scarred wizard's favorite dessert. And who wouldn't love such a sweet treat? Made of only a few ingredients, it doesn't take much time or hassle to conjure up a simply splendid treacle tart.

<u>Yield</u>
12 tarts

<u>Prep time</u>
30 minutes

<u>Cook time</u>
30 to 40 minutes

<u>Chill time</u>
1 hour

1¼ cups all-purpose flour
1 tablespoon granulated sugar
¼ teaspoon salt
5 tablespoons cold butter, cut into chunks
3 tablespoons vegetable shortening, chilled and cut into chunks
4 to 6 tablespoons ice water
1 cup honey
¼ cup heavy cream
1 cup fresh breadcrumbs
zest and juice of 1 lemon

1. Lightly grease the cups of a muffin tin with butter.
2. Put the flour, sugar, and salt in the bowl of a food processor.
3. Pulse the dry ingredients a few times to combine.
4. Scatter the butter and shortening over the flour mixture, and pulse several times until the mixture resembles coarse meal. There should be no powdery residue left.
5. Transfer the mixture to a large mixing bowl, and sprinkle the 4 to 6 tablespoons of cold water over the mixture to create a smooth dough.
6. Use a spatula to mix the batter with the water until it begins to clump together. If it's too dry, add more water, 1 tablespoon at a time. It's better for it to be a little too wet than too dry.
7. Gather the dough into a ball and divide it into 12 small discs. Wrap the discs in plastic wrap and refrigerate for an hour.
8. After the dough has chilled, remove it from the refrigerator and punch it out to soften it into a moldable texture. If the dough is sticky, add a tablespoon of flour. If it is dry, add a tablespoon of ice water.
9. Place one disc in each muffin cup, pressing it into the bottom and sides to create a crust cup. Or, if you prefer, you can roll the dough out and use a glass or jar with a large enough mouth to cut out discs that will be large enough to line the bottoms and sides of the muffin cups.
10. Preheat the oven to 375°F.
11. Mix together the honey, cream, breadcrumbs, lemon zest, and lemon juice in a bowl.
12. Once thoroughly mixed, pour the filling into the pie crusts.
13. Bake the tarts for 30 to 40 minutes, or until the filling is set. Remove from the oven and let cool for 5 minutes before serving.

Jam Doughnuts

The start-of-term feast is known for its over-the-top spread, so it's really no surprise that there are doughnuts among the other dessert offerings. Doughnuts can be a little tricky to make at home, but the warm, sugary results are totally worth the time and effort. Plus, this recipe utilizes the magic of store-bought jam, so the only thing you'll need to focus on is your doughnut dough.

Yield
12 to 14 doughnuts

Prep time
20 minutes

Rest time
3 hours

Cook time
16 to 24 minutes

3 cups plus 1 tablespoon all-purpose flour
¼ cup cane sugar, divided
2¼ teaspoons yeast
1½ cups plus 2 tablespoons water
¼ cup unsalted butter, melted
dash of salt
2 large egg yolks
jam of your choosing
frying oil
powdered sugar, for garnish

1. To a small mixing bowl, add the tablespoon of flour first, then the sugar on one side and the yeast on the other side to avoid them interacting directly.
2. Add the water. Mix well and cover. Let rest until the mixture becomes foamy, 10 minutes.
3. In a separate large mixing bowl, combine the remaining 3 cups of flour, melted butter, salt, remaining sugar, and egg yolks.
4. Slowly pour the yeast mixture into the flour mixture while stirring.
5. When the batter is smooth, cover the bowl with a clean tea towel and set aside in a warm spot to rise for 2 hours, until the dough has doubled in size.
6. After the batter has risen, punch it down and transfer it to a lightly floured surface. Roll out the dough into ¾-inch-thick rounds.
7. Use a glass or biscuit cutter to create circles approximately 2½ to 3 inches in diameter.
8. Spoon a dollop of jam into the middle of half of the circles of dough.
9. Cover the jam-filled circles with another circle of dough.
10. Pinch the edges of the circles together, all the way around, then cup your hands around the dough and form the filled pieces into balls, with the jam enclosed in the middle.
11. Cover the doughnuts again with a clean, slightly damp tea towel and let rise for 1 hour, until puffed.
12. Line a large platter or plate with several layers of paper towels and set aside.
13. Pour the frying oil into a deep-sided pan and bring the heat up to medium-high.

14. Once the oil has reached a deep-fry temperature of 350°F, start placing the doughnuts into the oil, working in small batches to prevent overcooking.
15. Fry the doughnuts on both sides until they're puffed and golden brown. This will take 2 to 3 minutes per side.
16. Remove them from the pan with a slotted spoon, draining off as much oil as possible. Transfer to the paper towel–lined plate to drain.
17. Cool slightly and then sprinkle with powdered sugar.
18. Serve and enjoy.

Tea at the Edge of the Forest

As the fall term progresses, life at the castle settles into a comforting routine. You've memorized your class schedule (and know which staircases to avoid at which times), you have your favorite teachers (all of the ones who *aren't* ghosts), and you're taking your favorite classes (potion making, anyone? No?). You also might have the privilege of being invited down to the Keeper of the Keys and Grounds' hut for afternoon tea. Though his baking can't compare to that of the house elves in the castle kitchen, it's the thought that counts, and time spent in that warm, cozy hut is always full of happiness, laughter, and, of course, magical creatures.

Bath Buns

Bath buns are a favorite in the non-magical world. They are often sprinkled with crushed sugar, and sometimes have a lump of sugar inside. This delightfully airy bun is perfect to nibble on while enjoying a cup of tea.

<u>Yield</u>
12 buns

<u>Prep time</u>
20 to 25 minutes, plus
2 hours, 45 minutes to rise

<u>Cook time</u>
20 to 25 minutes

1 stick unsalted butter,
room temperature
3⅓ cups all-purpose flour
2¼ teaspoons yeast
pinch of salt
9 tablespoons cane sugar, divided
1 cup plus 2 tablespoons
milk, divided
2 eggs, lightly whisked
1 tablespoon caraway seeds
pearl sugar or additional
caraway seeds, for garnish

1. In a large baking bowl, rub the butter into the flour.
2. Once you've got a crumbly mixture, add the yeast on one side of the bowl and the salt and sugar on the other side of the bowl to keep the yeast and salt separate. Stir thoroughly.
3. Add 1 cup of the milk to the lightly whisked eggs and stir together gently.
4. Pour the milk mixture into the flour mixture. Stir carefully.
5. Add the caraway seeds and stir again.
6. With either your hands or a wooden spoon, mix everything together really well to create a sticky dough.
7. Tip the dough out onto a lightly floured surface and knead for 6 to 8 minutes.
8. Transfer the dough to a large, covered bowl and set aside for 2 hours to double in size.
9. Line a baking sheet with parchment paper.
10. Once the dough has doubled in size, tip it back onto the floured surface and flatten it lightly into a round. Cut the dough into 12 equal pieces and roll each piece into a ball.
11. Place the 12 dough balls onto a baking sheet. Cover them with a damp tea towel and let rise again for 45 minutes.
12. Preheat the oven to 350°F.
13. To make the glaze, combine the remaining milk and sugar together and blend until thoroughly incorporated. Brush half of the glaze mixture over the buns and set aside the rest for later.
14. Bake the buns for 20 to 25 minutes, or until golden brown.
15. Remove from the oven and immediately place on a cooling rack or dry tea towel.
16. Brush on the remainder of the glaze while the buns are still warm, and sprinkle pearl sugar or caraway seeds on top of the buns.
17. Serve warm.

Rock Cakes

Rock cakes don't always have to be rock hard, despite what their name might suggest. Also called rock buns, these crumbly little cakes require less eggs and sugar than normal cake and often feature dried fruit. They are best served warm, with a cup of freshly brewed tea.

Yield
12 cakes

Prep time
10 minutes

Cook time
12 to 15 minutes

1½ cups all-purpose flour
1½ teaspoons baking powder
½ teaspoon pumpkin pie spice
6 tablespoons cold butter
⅓ cup cane sugar
1 egg
5 tablespoons milk
½ cup raisins

1. Preheat the oven to 425°F and line a baking sheet with parchment paper.
2. Sift together the flour, baking powder, and pumpkin pie spice in a medium bowl. Set aside.
3. With an electric handheld mixer, mix the butter and sugar to a mealy crumb texture.
4. Add the egg to the butter and sugar mixture, and beat until smooth.
5. Add the sifted flour mixture and milk.
6. Once it comes together, add in the raisins.
7. Mix until combined. Be careful not to overmix. The texture should be lumpy and seem almost a little dry.
8. With two forks, form the batter into lumpy cookies on the baking sheet, about 2 inches apart.
9. Place the baking sheet in the upper part of the oven and bake for 12 to 15 minutes, or until peaks start to turn brown.
10. Transfer from the oven to a cooling rack. Let cool for 10 to 20 minutes before serving.

Talonless Beef Casserole

Who knows what our favorite half-giant's casserole was actually made of—last time we checked, cows don't have talons. This recipe (though sans talon) is still full of meaty goodness and is perfect for a filling lunch on a brisk fall day.

Yield
6 servings

Prep time
15 minutes, plus time for making mashed potatoes

Cook time
40 to 45 minutes

1 pound ground beef
1½ cups green peas, lightly boiled, drained
2 to 3 medium carrots, sliced thin
1 small onion, chopped
1 teaspoon salt
2 teaspoons Italian seasoning
½ teaspoon freshly ground black pepper
handful of fresh cilantro leaves
4½ to 5 cups mashed potatoes
parsley flakes
olive oil

1. Preheat the oven to 400°F.
2. Preheat the cast-iron skillet on the stovetop over medium-high heat.
3. Once the skillet is hot, add the ground beef and brown.
4. Drain the fat from the beef and return it to the skillet.
5. Add the peas, carrots, onion, and spices, and stir together until thoroughly incorporated.
6. Sprinkle the cilantro leaves over the top of the meat and veggie mixture.
7. Now, layer the mashed potatoes over the top and press down with a spoon, turning the potatoes into a "crust."
8. Sprinkle the parsley flakes over the potatoes.
9. Drizzle the olive oil over the top of the potatoes and brush it across the top lightly with a pastry brush.
10. Put entire thing in the oven and bake for 40 to 45 minutes, or until the potatoes turn a light golden brown.
11. Remove from the oven and let stand for 2 to 3 minutes before serving.

Hallowe'en

We all know that Hallowe'en is an important holiday in the human world. After all, it's one of the few times humans can dress up as sorcerers and witches and not seem like they've gone batty. But Hallowe'en is also a favorite at Hogwarts, where the students and staff are always in for a spooky good time—unless there happens to be a troll in the dungeon! The Hallowe'en feast is pretty similar to the start-of-term feast save for a few additional goodies like Baked Pumpkin and Caramel Apple Slices. If you're looking to create a feast worthy of hundreds of floating jack-o'-lanterns and live bats, then pair up the start-of-term feast recipes with the ones following this intro. If you're looking for a more laid-back monster mash, the following recipes will be more than enough.

Carrot Cake

Carrot cake is a wonderful addition to any autumnal meal, or for any time of year. What's great about carrot cake is that you can tweak it to your own taste, take out the dried fruit, add some walnuts, put on extra frosting...it's all up to you. Make your cake a little more bedazzled by adding some cute carrot decorations.

Yield
24 small servings

Prep time
15 minutes

Cook time
1 hour, 20 minutes

2 cups sugar
1½ cups olive oil
1½ cups shredded carrots
12 ounces carrot baby food
3 cups all-purpose flour
2 teaspoons baking powder
2 teaspoons baking soda
1 teaspoon salt
2 teaspoons ground cinnamon
½ teaspoon ground nutmeg
4 eggs
½ cup pecans
powdered sugar, to top (optional)

Cream Cheese Frosting
½ cup butter, softened
8 ounces cream cheese, softened
4 cups powdered sugar
1 teaspoon vanilla extract

1. Preheat the oven to 350°F.
2. Prepare a Bundt cake pan (see notes) with a light coating of coconut spray.
3. In a medium mixing bowl, combine all ingredients, except for the eggs, pecans, and topping ingredients, until thoroughly combined.
4. Add in the eggs, one at a time. Mix together thoroughly.
5. Add the pecans and mix again until thoroughly combined.
6. Pour the batter into the prepared cake pan and bake for 1 hour, 20 minutes.
7. Cool on a rack for 2 hours before removing from the pan.
8. While the cake is cooling, make the Cream Cheese Frosting. In a medium bowl, combine the ingredients together. Beat until smooth and creamy.
9. When the cake is cool, sprinkle the top with powdered sugar or frost with the cream cheese frosting.

NOTES

The Bundt cake pan gives a delightful top to this cake. If possible, use one of these. If you prefer not to, an angel food cake pan is the second choice, or you can use a standard 9 x 13-inch pan.

Baked Pumpkin

It would be remiss of the house elves to exclude the most iconic squash of the season on the candy-strewn great hall tables. This recipe is quick and easy: simply cut up your pumpkin (and save the seeds for later toasting), spice it up, and put it in the oven to roast. You'll have a delicious fall dish in no time.

Yield
4 servings

Prep time
5 minutes

Cook time
20 minutes

1 small pumpkin or ¼ of a large pumpkin, seeded and sliced in 1-inch-thick slices

2 tablespoons olive oil

pinch of ground clove

1 teaspoon ground cinnamon

¼ teaspoon ground nutmeg

1 teaspoon sea salt

2 tablespoons packed brown sugar

feta, seeds, and chopped parsley, for topping (optional)

1. Preheat the oven to 400°F.
2. Place the slices of pumpkin on a baking sheet. Drizzle olive oil on the pumpkin and use a pastry brush to coat the slices with oil.
3. Next, sprinkle the seasonings and sugar on the slices.
4. Place the sheet in the oven and bake for 20 minutes or until the edges start to turn dark golden brown.
5. Remove from the oven and let cool for 5 minutes. To serve, top with feta, seeds, and chopped parsley, if desired.

Cockroach Clusters

These might sound a bit too creepy-crawly for some, but they're made up of crowd-pleasing ingredients like pecans, chocolate, and marshmallows.

Yield
36 clusters

Prep time
5 minutes

Cook time
7 to 12 minutes

Chill time
4 hours

12 ounces semisweet
chocolate chips
2 tablespoons unsalted butter
3 tablespoons milk
¼ cup pecan halves
½ cup miniature marshmallows
3 tablespoons shredded coconut

1. Line a baking sheet with parchment paper.
2. In a double boiler, combine the chocolate and butter over medium heat. Stir constantly to avoid burning.
3. Once the chocolate is quickly melting, 3 to 5 minutes, bring the heat down to low. Continue stirring.
4. Add the milk and stir together until smooth, 2 minutes. Remove from the heat.
5. Stir in the pecans, marshmallows, and coconut. Stir until everything is thoroughly coated in chocolate, 2 to 3 minutes.
6. Spoon out 1 tablespoon of the mixture onto the parchment paper. Be sure to leave a little room between each candy.
7. Place in the refrigerator and chill for 4 hours.

Caramel Apple Slices

These caramel apple slices are perfect for a party, and much easier to eat than a whole caramel apple. Plus, with slices, you're able to customize the toppings! Try chocolate, crushed nuts, or coconut. It's hard to go wrong with such a classic.

Yield
15 slices

Prep time
20 minutes

Cook time
5 minutes

5 medium green and red apples, cored and cut into 1-inch slices
1 pound caramel
2 tablespoons cream
⅔ cup semisweet chocolate chips
3 teaspoons vegetable oil, divided
⅔ cup milk chocolate chips
⅔ cup white chocolate chips
juice of 1 lemon
¼ cup coconut shavings
½ cup peanuts or other nut of your choice, chopped
15 pointed wooden skewers

1. Stick a wooden skewer into each apple slice.
2. Combine the caramel and cream in a microwave-safe bowl. Microwave on high in 30-second increments, stirring between each increment, until the caramel and cream are fully melted and combined.
3. Melt the semisweet chocolate chips with 1 teaspoon of oil in a microwave-safe bowl for 15-second increments, stirring every 15 seconds until melted.
4. Melt the milk chocolate chips with 1 teaspoon of oil in a microwave-safe bowl for 15-second increments, stirring every 15 seconds until melted.
5. Melt the white chocolate chips with 1 teaspoon of oil in a microwave-safe bowl for 15-second increments, stirring every 15 seconds until melted.
6. If you don't want your apples to brown, brush them with lemon juice.
7. Dip the slices into the melted caramel or chocolate, letting the excess drip off. Place on a waxed paper–lined baking sheet to set.
8. Repeat until all the slices are coated in caramel or chocolate.
9. Dust with coconut shavings or chopped nuts.

A Ghostly Deathday Party

Throughout your time at school, you may find
yourself making friends with some ghosts. You
might even find yourself invited to a Deathday
Party on Hallowe'en, though it means missing
the feast in the great hall for a rather sickening
spread of moldy and rotting food. For those
who do the right thing and attend in support
of their friend (and even for those who are just
dragged along), here are some palatable recipes
to make a night of musical saws and gloomy,
dancing nuns that much more memorable.

Baked Fish

If you're planning on celebrating your own Deathday, it's important to have an eye-catching centerpiece for the meal. Our favorite nearly headless ghost chose to put his main dish of rotten fish on fancy silver platters. This recipe swaps out rotten fish for fresh. After all, if you're going to invite guests who are still alive, it's best to have some food that they can eat too.

Yield
4 servings

Prep time
20 to 25 minutes

Cook time
24 to 27 minutes

1 egg
4 small red potatoes, chopped
2 small white onions, chopped
½ pound fresh fennel, chopped, fronds reserved
2 lemons, sliced
8 fresh cherry tomatoes, halved
handful of pitted olives
2 cloves garlic, peeled and chopped
4 trout or whitefish, heads and tails intact
olive oil
salt and pepper, to taste
1 teaspoon dill
juice of 1 lemon

1. Preheat the oven to 375°F.
2. Create a bag for your fish by folding up aluminum foil into a sort of envelope, using egg to seal the seams, or use a brown paper bag, whichever you prefer. Leave one side open. Set aside.
3. In a large pot, bring 6 cups water with a pinch of salt to a gentle boil.
4. Place the potatoes in the water and cook for 6 to 7 minutes. Drain and let cool while you prepare the other vegetables.
5. Add the fennel, lemon slices, cherry tomatoes, olives, and garlic to a bowl with the cooled potatoes and the fish.
6. Lightly stream olive oil over everything.
7. Season with salt, pepper, and dill.
8. Add the lemon juice.
9. Toss everything together lightly to coat.
10. Transfer all of the ingredients into your foil or paper bag.
11. Sprinkle in the reserved fennel fronds.
12. Place the bag on a baking tray and place the tray in the oven.
13. Bake for 18 to 20 minutes, or until the potatoes and fish are thoroughly cooked.
14. To serve, place the bag on a serving platter and gently pierce it to release the steam. Dish out individual servings, including the sauce, from the bag, and serve with a side of your preferred vegetables, such as green beans or broccoli.

Haggis-Inspired Stew

Haggis is a traditional dish made of several very interesting ingredients, like sheep's lung. Since some of these ingredients are not available (and actually illegal) in the United States, this recipe is a stew inspired by the hearty, savory flavors that can be found in haggis.

<u>Yield</u>
6 to 8 servings

<u>Prep time</u>
20 minutes

<u>Cook time</u>
1 hour (pressure cooker)
or 6 hours (slow cooker)

<u>Rest time (optional)</u>
1 hour

1½ pounds stewing beef
¼ cup all-purpose flour
1½ teaspoons freshly
ground black pepper
1½ teaspoons salt
1 tablespoon garlic powder
2 bay leaves
2 teaspoons paprika
2 teaspoons Worcestershire sauce
1 onion, chopped
3 potatoes, chopped
1 stalk celery, chopped
4 carrots, sliced
1½ cups beef stock
1 cup water
parsley or fresh herbs, for garnish

1. Rinse the meat thoroughly and place it in the slow cooker or Instant Pot.
2. In a small bowl, mix together the flour, ground pepper, and salt.
3. Once mixed, dump the flour mix into the pot with the meat and stir together, coating the meat with the flour mix.
4. Stir in the remaining dry seasonings along with the Worcestershire sauce, onion, potatoes, celery, and carrots. Mix together.
5. Pour in the beef stock and water, and mix again until everything is coated and the stock and water have blended.
6. Cover the pot.
7. If using a slow cooker, put on high heat for 6 hours. If using an Instant Pot or similar electric pressure cooker, use the stew setting. After the stew has cooked on this setting for 1 hour, vent the steam and, if desired, let it sit for another hour on simmer or the keep-warm setting.
8. Serve hot, topped with parsley or fresh herbs of choice.

Birthday Red Velvet Cake with Gray Icing

It's not a Deathday party without a celebratory cake! The Deathday boy's cake was a great behemoth of a thing, shaped like a tombstone and frosted with gray icing. Though this recipe uses circular cake pans (which are more accessible), feel free to carve your cake into any spooky shape you desire. Don't forget to write your name and death date on top!

Yield
10 to 12 slices

Prep time
20 minutes

Cook time
30 to 35 minutes

2½ cups all-purpose flour
1⅓ cups cane sugar
2½ tablespoons unsweetened cocoa powder
1 teaspoon baking soda
1 teaspoon salt
1½ cups buttermilk or buttermilk substitute
2 large egg whites
1 tablespoon red food coloring
1 teaspoon white vinegar
1½ teaspoons vanilla extract
1 cup unsweetened applesauce
Gray Icing (page 75)
½ cup pecan halves (optional)

1. Preheat the oven to 350°F.
2. Lightly coat three (6-inch-diameter) round cake pans with olive or coconut oil cooking spray.
3. In a large mixing bowl, use a whisk to combine the flour, sugar, cocoa powder, baking soda, and salt. Whisk until completely incorporated.
4. In a separate mixing bowl, combine buttermilk or buttermilk substitute (see notes), egg whites, food coloring, vinegar, and vanilla extract, and whisk together thoroughly.
5. Add the applesauce to the liquid mix, ½ cup at a time. Blend thoroughly and add the second ½ cup.
6. Pour the liquid mixture into the dry mixture. Stir completely until a batter forms and the lumps are gone. The batter will be textured, however, thanks to the applesauce.
7. Pour the batter into the pans and place them on the lower rack in the oven. Bake the cake for 30 to 35 minutes or until a toothpick inserted into the center comes out clean.
8. Cool the cake completely in its pans, then remove from the pans.
9. Ice the top of one of the cake rounds with Gray Icing.
10. Place an unfrosted cake round on the frosted one. Frost with the icing.
11. Repeat with the third cake round, icing both the top and sides.
12. Place the pecan halves on the top and sides of the cake, if desired.

Gray Icing

½ cup butter, softened
8 ounces cream cheese, softened
1 teaspoon vanilla extract
3 cups powdered sugar, sifted
red and green food coloring

1. Combine the butter and cream cheese with an electric handheld mixer until completely smooth. Scrape down the sides.
2. Beat in the vanilla extract.
3. Add the powdered sugar, 1 cup at a time, beating together with the butter mixture until completely blended and smooth. Set aside.
4. Add the red and green food coloring in equal parts and mix until you create a flat gray. Continue to add 3 or 4 drops at a time of both colors until the desired shade is reached (see notes).

NOTES

• Buttermilk substitute is easy to make. In a measuring cup, place 1½ tablespoons of white vinegar. Fill the remainder of the space with milk. Stir together and let sit for 5 minutes before using.

• Measure the food coloring drops out into a spoon. Then stir the drops into the icing. It's easier to control the number of drops if you use this method, rather than adding the food coloring drops directly to the icing. For a dark gray icing, add in several drops of each color. For a light gray, add in just a few drops of each color.

Winter Recipes

Though Hogwarts is always magical no matter what the season, wintertime at the castle always holds a special kind of enchantment. The grounds are covered with fresh snow, the Great Lake is frozen solid, and the castle is decorated to the nines. Twelve towering fir trees fill the great hall with their fresh pine scent, candles and snowflakes float above the tables, and giant Christmas ornaments gleam in the light. Even the suits of armor are in a festive spirit, singing carols to passersby.

Students who stay on at the castle during the holidays are in for a treat. For our favorite bespectacled boy (who gets a single tissue and dog biscuits, among other things, for Christmas from his blood relatives), the winter holidays at Hogwarts are absolutely spectacular. He gets real presents! He gets to spend time with his best friends! And, of course, he gets to partake in the most wondrous Christmas dinner.

Christmas

After waking up to real presents and spending time with your best friend, it's hard to imagine how Christmas Day could get any better. This is where the Christmas feast comes in. It's the perfect ending to a perfect holiday, filled with a plethora of dishes, drinks, and, of course, wizard poppers that explode with magical surprises inside. These recipes are all traditional classics, best served with good cheer and a paper crown on your head. Happy Christmas!

Crumpets

Crumpets are the perfect thing to have for breakfast on Christmas morning, and students who stay at the castle during the holidays tend to do exactly that. Melt some butter over your crumpets and serve them while they're hot—delicious!

Yield
10 crumpets

Prep time
15 minutes, plus 1 hour,
40 minutes to rest

Cook time
10 to 12 minutes

1 teaspoon cane sugar
1 tablespoon yeast
1 cup warm milk
2 cups all-purpose flour
1 teaspoon salt
½ teaspoon baking soda
1 cup warm water

1. In a medium mixing bowl, stir together the sugar, yeast, and warm milk. Let the mixture rest for 10 minutes, until it becomes frothy.
2. In a separate large bowl, combine the flour and salt.
3. Once the milk mixture has frothed, pour it into the flour mixture and work together with a spatula until a thick dough forms.
4. Cover the bowl loosely with plastic wrap and let it stand in a warm place for 1 hour, allowing the dough to rise to nearly double its size.
5. Once the dough has risen, dissolve the baking soda into the warm water in a small bowl. Once it is combined, add it to the dough and beat it and the dough together for a few minutes. The dough will be lumpy.
6. Cover the dough and let it rest for another 30 minutes to rise again and get bubbly. Once the dough has risen, preheat your cast-iron skillet over medium heat. Prepare the crumpet rings (see notes) by oiling the inside of each rim.
7. Once the skillet has warmed, add a little bit of oil to the pan. Place the rings on the skillet, bringing the heat up to medium-high.
8. Once the rings are hot, pour the batter into each ring, filling them about halfway.
9. Cook the crumpets for 8 to 10 minutes, or until they're solid, the tops are cooked and have formed pores, and the bottoms are lightly browned.
10. Remove the rings and flip the crumpets, cooking for another 2 minutes to lightly brown the tops. Or, if you plan to serve later, leave the tops unbrowned and toast them instead when you're ready to serve.

NOTES
If you can't get hold of actual crumpet rings, use biscuit cutters, round cookie cutters, or anything else similar.

Roast Turkey

A golden roast turkey is a must for any traditional Christmas dinner. Though these birds can be a little tricky, especially if you don't have the help of a magic wand or a house elf, don't be afraid to give one a try.

<u>Yield</u>
approximately 1 serving per pound of turkey

<u>Prep time</u>
15 minutes

<u>Cook time</u>
varies

<u>Herb Butter Mix</u>
8 tablespoons soft butter
¼ cup cilantro leaves, finely chopped, stems removed
4 cloves garlic, finely chopped or minced
½ teaspoon sea salt
½ teaspoon freshly ground black pepper

<u>Roast Turkey</u>
½ cup olive oil, divided
2 oranges, sliced, divided
2 lemons, sliced, divided
½ teaspoon garlic powder
½ teaspoon minced onion
¼ teaspoon sea salt, plus more as indicated
¼ teaspoon freshly ground black pepper, plus more as indicated
½ teaspoon dried parsley flakes
1 (12- to 16-pound) turkey
6 to 8 cloves garlic

1. Preheat the oven to the appropriate temperature based on the chart on page 84.
2. Blend all of the herb butter mix ingredients together until the spices and herbs are thoroughly mixed into the butter. Set aside.
3. Line a large roasting pan with aluminum foil, then spread ¼ cup of olive oil as evenly as possible throughout the pan.
4. Lay out the slices from 1 orange and 1 lemon throughout the pan, again, as evenly as possible.
5. Sprinkle the garlic powder, minced onion, sea salt, ground pepper, and parsley flakes throughout the pan and into the oil and citrus base.
6. Remove the organs from the turkey cavity if they have been left inside the bird. Thoroughly rinse the bird with warm water and pat it dry with either a couple of paper towels or a tea towel.
7. Place the turkey breast-side down into the pan.
8. Stuff the garlic cloves into the bird's cavity. Be sure to split up and peel the garlic so that the garlic can spread throughout the bird.
9. Stuff the slices of 1 orange and 1 lemon inside the turkey.
10. To prevent the skin from burning or drying out, use a fork to rub half of the herb butter mix on the turkey's skin, coating as much of the skin with the butter as possible. It will be lumpy, but that's okay.
11. Drizzle the second ¼ cup of olive oil over the turkey.
12. Lightly dust the turkey with salt and pepper to simply boost the flavor a bit. Cover the turkey and place it in the oven.
13. Set a timer and roast the turkey for approximately half the designated time from the chart on page 84.
14. Pull the turkey out and turn it over with clean towels, heatproof gloves, or oven mitts so that it is breast-side up.
15. Using a fork, slather the remainder of the herb butter mix over the breast of the turkey, and lightly sprinkle additional salt and pepper over the skin. The butter will melt quickly due to the heat, so don't worry about lumps.

16. Reduce the heat of the oven to either 325°F for standard ovens or 300°F for fan-forced ovens.

17. Baste the bird with pan juices and cover. Roast for an additional hour.

18. Baste the bird once more, cover, and roast for another 30 minutes.

19. After 30 minutes, baste the bird one last time with pan juices, leaving it uncovered as you return it to cook. Roast the turkey for the remainder of the time until the "pop-up" indicator pops.

20. Insert a meat thermometer between the breast and leg to test the internal temperature. It should read 165°F (75°C).

21. If the temperature is right, remove the bird from the oven and let it cool for 5 to 7 minutes before transferring it to the serving platter. If the temperature is not correct, baste the bird again and return it to the oven, uncovered, for another 20 to 30 minutes.

22. Repeat this process, if necessary, until the bird reaches the proper temperature to safely serve.

NOTES

If you like extra-crispy skin, broil the turkey for the last 5 to 10 minutes of cook time. Keep a close eye on the bird, though, to make sure it doesn't burn. If you notice the bird is browning too quickly, loosely tent some aluminum foil over the pan.

TURKEY ROASTING CHARTS

Different types of ovens require different temperatures when it comes to roasting a turkey. Depending on their size, turkeys also require varying lengths of time to cook. This chart should help you figure out how to accommodate both oven type and turkey size as you prepare this winter feast.

Oven Chart

Fan-forced ovens: 390°F (200°C)   Standard ovens: 425°F (220°C)

Turkey Size Chart

Remember that these are approximate times. Factors such as altitude and accuracy of your oven temperatures will determine precise times.

10 pounds	2 hours, 15 minutes
12 pounds	2 hours, 35 to 45 minutes
14 pounds	3 hours
16 pounds	3 hours, 15 to 20 minutes
18 pounds	3 hours, 45 to 55 minutes
20 pounds	4 hours, 15 to 20 minutes

Leftover Turkey Sandwiches

After all the work you put into roasting your own turkey, do not let those leftovers go to waste! These sandwiches are so good they will have you reliving Christmas Day all over again.

Yield
1 sandwich

Prep time
5 minutes

cream cheese
2 slices whole wheat
or light rye bread
leftover turkey
leftover stuffing
leftover cranberry sauce
handful of fresh spinach

1. Smear some cream cheese on 1 slice of bread.
2. Lay on a thick layer of leftover turkey.
3. Add a helping of stuffing.
4. Layer on some cranberry sauce.
5. Add a handful of fresh spinach and top with the second slice of bread.
6. Press down lightly to help the sandwich stay together.
7. Serve immediately.

NOTES
If you don't have enough stuffing and cranberry sauce to go around, you can skip these ingredients and trade them out for a simple change: ranch dressing. The ranch with the cream cheese, spinach, and turkey is a simple but delicious dressed-down option.

Chipolatas

Chipolatas, or fresh pork sausages, are a staple of an English Christmas dinner, no matter if it's a wizarding or a non-magical feast. This recipe includes a few extra ingredients along with the sausages to pack in more flavor.

Yield
6 servings

Prep time
10 minutes, plus 2 hours to marinate

Cook time
30 to 40 minutes

10 to 12 ounces cocktail sausages

4 strips uncooked bacon, cut to bits

4½ tablespoons maple syrup

¼ cup pineapple juice

¼ cup pineapple chunks

1. Place all of the ingredients in an oven-safe pan.
2. Cover the pan with foil and marinate for 2 hours.
3. Preheat the oven to 400°F.
4. Uncover the pan and place it in the oven. Bake for 30 to 40 minutes or until the bacon crisps.
5. Remove the pan from the oven and let the sausages cool for 1 to 2 minutes.
6. Serve hot.

Cranberry Sauce

You can't have roast turkey without cranberry sauce. While everyone has their preference, whether canned or homemade, this recipe is sure to be a crowd-pleaser, thanks to some added citrusy brightness from orange and lemon.

<u>Yield</u>
11 servings

<u>Prep time</u>
5 minutes

<u>Cook time</u>
25 minutes

1 cup orange juice
1 cup cane sugar
12 ounces fresh cranberries
zest of 1 lemon
zest of 1 orange

1. In a medium saucepan over medium-low heat, warm the orange juice and sugar until the sugar dissolves.
2. Once the sugar is thoroughly dissolved, stir in the cranberries and citrus fruit zest.
3. Stir the cranberries constantly until the berries start popping.
4. Once the majority of the cranberries have popped, remove the pan from the heat.
5. Transfer everything into a heat-resistant bowl.
6. Chill overnight.

NOTES
Technically, you don't need to chill the sauce overnight, as it will gel and solidify simply from cooling down. It will have a nicer, firmer texture, however, if it is allowed to chill for longer before serving.

Christmas Pudding

Christmas pudding dates all the way back to Hogwarts' founding, and perhaps even earlier! Many families have their own secret recipes for this traditional holiday dish, also known as plum pudding, so we can assume that the castle kitchen makes a very special one for the students and staff.

Yield
10 servings

Prep time
15 minutes

Cook time
3½ to 4 hours

1 cup raisins
1 cup chopped dried apricots
1½ cups all-purpose flour
1½ teaspoons baking soda
¼ teaspoon salt
1 cup finely grated butter, plus more to butter the pudding mold and aluminum foil
1 cup fresh brown breadcrumbs
1 cup light-brown sugar
1 cup mixed nuts
1 teaspoon ground cinnamon
¼ teaspoon ground allspice
¼ teaspoon ground nutmeg
¼ teaspoon ground cloves
¼ teaspoon ground ginger
¼ teaspoon ground coriander
1 cup milk
1 large egg
Butterscotch Sauce (page 89)

1. Use a pan with a wider circumference than your pudding mold and fill it halfway with water. Place it on the stovetop over low heat to simmer while you prepare the pudding.
2. Butter the inside of the pudding mold and set aside.
3. Combine the dried fruit, flour, baking soda, salt, butter, breadcrumbs, sugar, nuts, and spices in a large mixing bowl. Thoroughly coat everything, allowing the butter to smear into the rest of the ingredients.
4. Add the milk and egg. Combine the ingredients together until they are well incorporated. Pour the mixture into the pudding mold.
5. Cut two squares of aluminum foil large enough to cover the top of the pudding mold.
6. Butter the inside sheets of the foil and place both layers over the mold. Create a crease in the middle of the foil to make space for the pudding to rise properly.
7. Gently place the pudding mold into the simmering water. The water should come up to about halfway on the mold. If it doesn't, add more water until it does.
8. Steam the pudding for 3½ to 4 hours, with the foil tightly in place. Check the water level throughout the steaming process and top it up if too much evaporates.
9. Once the pudding is solid enough to flip out of the pan onto a plate, you can either serve it immediately or let it cool for 10 minutes before wrapping it in cling wrap and new foil and placing it in the refrigerator.
10. Pour Butterscotch Sauce over the pudding to serve.

Butterscotch Sauce

5 tablespoons butter
½ cup packed brown sugar
¾ cup heavy whipping cream
1 teaspoon vanilla extract

1. Combine all of the ingredients in a saucepan over medium heat and slowly bring to a boil. Let boil for 2 to 3 minutes, stirring constantly.
2. Remove from the heat when the sugar is fully dissolved and the sauce is a pale caramel color and slightly thickened.

Eggnog

This is a recipe for creamy, traditional eggnog, which is almost a meal in and of itself! There is no alcohol in this recipe, but if you'd like to spike yours with rum, you'll find no judgment here!

<u>Yield</u>
8 servings

<u>Prep time</u>
15 minutes

<u>Chill time</u>
1 hour

4 eggs, yolks and whites separated
⅓ cup plus 1 tablespoon cane sugar, divided
4 cups milk
1 cup heavy whipping cream
1 teaspoon ground cinnamon
1 teaspoon ground nutmeg
1½ teaspoons vanilla extract

1. Beat the egg yolks with an electric handheld mixer at low speed for 2 minutes.
2. Add ⅓ cup of sugar, milk, and cream, and blend until combined thoroughly.
3. Add the spices and blend on low until combined thoroughly.
4. In a separate bowl, beat the egg whites until soft peaks form. Gradually add the remaining 1 tablespoon sugar to the egg whites while continuously beating, and continue beating until stiff peaks form.
5. Add the vanilla extract to the yolk mixture and whisk together until incorporated.
6. Add the egg whites and whisk together until thoroughly blended.
7. Chill for 1 hour and serve.

Trifle

Here's another trifle recipe, this time with a peppermint chocolate twist. This dessert will ensure a bewitchingly festive end to any Christmas dinner!

Yield
20 servings

Prep time
15 to 20 minutes

2 (8-inch) rounds Chocolate Gâteau recipe (page 49), without the filling or frosting
4 cups vanilla pudding
1 package Oreos, broken to pieces
1 tub whipped cream
candy canes, for garnish

1. Cut the cooled cake into cubes.
2. Place 2 cups of pudding into the bottom of a large trifle bowl, glass bowl, or glass vase—or a few tablespoons into individual tall glasses.
3. Layer in some broken Oreos.
4. Add a layer of whipped cream topping.
5. Repeat the pudding, Oreo, and whipped cream layers. The top layer should be whipped cream, candy cane garnishes, and crumbled Oreo bits.

An Owl-Mail Christmas Cake

You can always count on the woman who's raised seven ginger children to send yummy surprises via owl mail. The Christmas cake she sent in the holiday care package was no doubt received much better than the maroon jumper. This recipe combines the yummiest flavors of the season in a portable loaf cake—key for transport (mail owls need as much help as they can get!).

Yield
10 servings

Prep time
15 minutes

Cook time
45 to 50 minutes

2 cups all-purpose flour
1 teaspoon baking soda
1½ teaspoons ground ginger
¾ teaspoon ground nutmeg
½ teaspoon salt
¼ cup cane sugar
½ cup butter, softened
½ cup molasses
1 teaspoon vanilla extract
2 eggs
1 cup buttermilk
½ cup pecans or walnuts
(optional), plus more for garnish

Drizzle
1½ cups powdered sugar
¼ teaspoon vanilla extract
5 to 5½ teaspoons milk

1. Preheat the oven to 350°F.
2. In a large mixing bowl, combine the flour, baking soda, ginger, nutmeg, and salt. Set aside.
3. In a separate large mixing bowl, combine the sugar and butter until thoroughly combined and creamy.
4. Add the molasses and vanilla to the sugar mixture, and blend until completely incorporated.
5. Add the eggs to the sugar mixture, one at a time, until thoroughly combined.
6. Alternate adding the flour mixture and buttermilk to the sugar mixture. Stir each mixture completely before adding the next one.
7. Add the nuts, if desired, and mix until they're completely incorporated.
8. Spoon the batter into a greased loaf pan and bake for 45 to 50 minutes.
9. Cool in the pan for 10 minutes, then remove to a baking rack to finish cooling.
10. While the cake is cooling, combine all the drizzle ingredients in a mixing bowl and stir until smooth and flowing, perfect for drizzling.
11. Pour the drizzle over the cooled cake, then garnish with additional nuts, if desired.

Christmas Care Package Nut Brittle

Another care package tradition, nut brittle, is the perfect treat to snack on as you wait for Christmas dinner to be served in the great hall. This recipe is quick and easy, and makes enough brittle to share with all of your friends.

Yield
12 to 16 servings

Prep time
5 minutes

Cook time
10 to 15 minutes

1 cup granulated sugar
½ cup light corn syrup
¼ teaspoon salt
¼ cup water
1 cup unsalted nuts
2 tablespoons unsalted butter, softened
1 teaspoon vanilla extract
1 teaspoon baking soda

1. Line a baking sheet with parchment paper. Set aside.
2. Gather and portion out all ingredients carefully to avoid possible burning during cooking time.
3. In a 2-quart saucepan over medium heat, bring the sugar, corn syrup, salt, and water to a boil. Stir until the sugar is dissolved.
4. Add the nuts and stir until combined.
5. Put a candy thermometer into the mixture and continue cooking, stirring constantly, until the temperature reaches 300°F.
6. Immediately remove the saucepan from the heat, and quickly stir in the butter, vanilla, and baking soda.
7. Immediately pour the mixture onto the prepared baking sheet.
8. Use a rubber spatula to spread the mixture out on the sheet as evenly as possible.
9. Cool the brittle completely at room temperature.
10. Snap the candy into pieces and serve as desired. Store in an airtight container at room temperature.

Yule Ball

Get out your dress robes and make sure your beautification charms are perfect, because it's time for the Yule Ball—and this grand celebration happens only every five years. After head-banging to some entrancing rock and roll and performing some professor-approved waltzing, you'll be hungry for refreshments. The following recipes have been selected to pay homage to the visiting schools, with some iconic dishes from all their countries.

Bouillabaisse

Sure to make any part-Veela smile, this bouillabaisse recipe is traditional, yet still easy enough to make in a home cook's kitchen. Feel free to add in your own favorite seafood to really make this recipe your own.

Yield
10 to 12 servings

Prep time
15 minutes

Cook time
38 to 40 minutes

9 cups water
5 pounds mixed seafood
(fish, shrimp, scallops, crabs,
mussels, clams, or other)
¾ pound mussels, cleaned
and debearded
1 bay leaf
12 black peppercorns
peel of 1 orange
¾ cup high-quality olive oil
2 small white onions,
thinly sliced
2 leeks, sliced
2 fennel sprigs
4 cloves garlic, minced
3 large tomatoes, peeled,
seeded, and chopped
1 cup dry white wine
2 sprigs fresh thyme, divided
1 tablespoon coarse sea salt
pinch of saffron threads
2 to 4 sprigs flat-leaf
parsley, chopped
1 baguette, sliced ½-inch thin

1. Bone the fish, peel the shrimp, remove the shells from the scallops and crabs, reserving the crustacean shells and collecting the other ingredients together.
2. Bring the water to a simmer and toss in the shells of any crustaceans, along with the bay leaf, peppercorns, and orange peel. Continue simmering for 15 minutes.
3. While everything is simmering, heat the olive oil over medium heat in a soup pan.
4. Add the onions, leeks, and fennel, along with a pinch of salt, to the olive oil. Slowly sweat the ingredients until they're tender but not browned.
5. Add the garlic, sautéing it until tender and fragrant.
6. Add the tomatoes and wine.
7. Turn up the heat until the wine begins to boil. Cook until the wine is reduced by half.
8. Strain the shrimp shell and orange mixture into the onion mixture.
9. Add 1 sprig of thyme, sea salt, saffron, and parsley, and simmer for 10 minutes.
10. Add the fish first.
11. After about 2 minutes, add the mussels and any clams or scallops.
12. About 2 minutes after that, add in the shrimp.
13. Simmer everything together until the shrimp is just cooked through. This should take 2 to 3 minutes.
14. Remove from the heat and serve immediately with a sliced baguette, garnishing with the remaining thyme.

Goulash

This is a more Americanized version of the dish that originated in medieval Hungary. Though the ingredients are accessible for an everyday meal, the results are sure to satisfy even a very talented sports star after a long night of dancing.

Yield
6 servings

Prep time
10 minutes

Cook time
30 minutes

1 pound ground turkey
2 medium onions, chopped
4 cloves garlic, chopped
4 large carrots, chopped
1 teaspoon plus 1 dash
of salt, divided
8 ounces macaroni
1 (14.5-ounce) can
crushed tomatoes
1 (14.5-ounce) can
diced tomatoes
½ teaspoon ground pepper
3 or 4 stems fresh parsley,
chopped, plus more for garnish
2 teaspoons dried basil
3 teaspoons dried oregano
1 bell pepper (any
color), chopped

1. Preheat a cast-iron skillet on the stovetop over medium heat. Once the pan is heated, add the ground turkey.
2. Brown the meat for 5 to 7 minutes and drain the fat.
3. Place the pan with the meat back on the stove, and add the onions, garlic, carrots, and teaspoon of salt. Cook for 5 to 7 minutes, or until the onions are translucent.
4. Fill a large saucepot with water and add a dash of salt. Bring the water to a boil.
5. Reduce the heat under the meat to low, and cover the pan with a lid while the water is boiling.
6. Add the macaroni to the water and cook to al dente.
7. Remove the pasta from the heat and drain. Return the pasta to the saucepot over low heat.
8. Add the meat mixture to the saucepot with the noodles.
9. Add the crushed tomatoes and diced tomatoes to the pot.
10. Add the pepper and dried herbs, stirring until they are thoroughly incorporated.
11. Add the bell pepper.
12. Simmer on low heat for 5 minutes or until warm.
13. Garnish with fresh parsley and serve immediately.

Shrimp Cocktail

Shrimp cocktail is a perfect appetizer for any fancy party or ball, plus it's super simple to make.

Yield
6 servings

Prep time
20 to 25 minutes

Cook time
5 to 7 minutes

Chill time
1-plus hours

6 cups water
1 tablespoon salt
¼ cup cane sugar
2 lemons
12 ounces precooked shrimp, thawed or fresh, deveined, tails on
8 cups ice

Cocktail Sauce
½ cup ketchup
juice of ¼ lemon
1 tablespoons horseradish sauce
¼ teaspoon garlic powder
½ teaspoon freshly ground black pepper

1. Add the water, salt, and sugar to a large saucepan over medium-high heat.
2. Cut lemons in half and juice. Pour the juice into the pan and place the lemon halves in the pan.
3. Bring the water to a gentle boil, dissolving the sugar and salt completely.
4. Remove the pan from the heat and put the shrimp in the pan, leaving them there, uncovered, for 3 to 4 minutes.
5. Once the shrimp are done poaching, immediately dump the ice into the pot with the shrimp to chill them rapidly.
6. Let the shrimp sit in the ice for 10 to 15 minutes.
7. Drain the shrimp and pat them dry with a paper towel.
8. Cover and chill until they are ready to serve, preferably 1-plus hours.
9. Make the cocktail sauce; combine the ingredients together, in order, and mix them thoroughly until they are fully incorporated. Chill for 1-plus hours and serve with the shrimp.

Blancmange

Blancmange is an impressive dessert, mostly thanks to its shape. It's nice to have a fancy mold on hand so your blancmange can look worthy of the Yule Ball, but if you only have a plain Bundt pan, that's fine, too. This recipe is for a blancmange that tastes even better than it looks!

Yield
6 servings

Prep time
5 minutes

Cook time
15 minutes

Set time
6 hours

3 cups milk, divided
peel of 1 lemon, cut into strips
2 cinnamon sticks
¼ cup cornstarch
½ cup cane sugar
ground cinnamon
lemon or orange
marmalade, to serve

1. Place 1 cup of milk into a saucepan.
2. Add the lemon peel and cinnamon sticks.
3. Turn the heat up to medium and bring the milk to a simmer.
4. Meanwhile, in a small bowl, whisk together the cornstarch and sugar.
5. Whisk the remaining milk into the cornstarch mixture.
6. Once the milk in the pan has begun to simmer, pour the cornstarch mixture into the heated milk in a slow, steady stream.
7. Turn the heat up slightly. Continuously whisk everything together until the mixture comes to a gentle boil.
8. Let boil for 20 seconds, continuously whisking.
9. Remove the pan from the heat.
10. Remove the lemon peel and cinnamon sticks with a slotted spoon.
11. Pour the mixture into a mold or silicone pan, and sprinkle ground cinnamon over the top.
12. Chill for 6 hours to fully set before serving.
13. Serve with the lemon or orange marmalade as a topping.

New Year's

New Year's tends to blend in with the Christmas holiday at the castle, but we can imagine that the wizarding world puts on some fiendishly festive celebrations. Just think of the enchanted fireworks that the twins set off during fifth year— and that wasn't even for a New Year's celebration! The recipes in this section are inspired by the twins' mother, who always sends a treat-filled care package during the winter holidays.

Chocolate Fudge

Delicious homemade fudge was part of our favorite protagonist's first-year Christmas haul. Here is a recipe that is worthy of celebrating both Christmas and New Year. It includes nuts, but these are completely optional.

Yield
30 pieces of fudge

Prep time
10 minutes

Cook time
5 minutes

Chill time
2 hours

coconut oil cooking spray
3 cups semisweet chocolate chips
1 (14-ounce) can sweetened condensed milk
pinch of salt
1½ teaspoons vanilla extract
1 cup chopped pecans or nuts of choice (optional)

1. Lightly coat an 8-inch square glass baking dish with coconut oil cooking spray.
2. In a medium saucepan over low heat, stir together the chocolate chips, sweetened condensed milk, and salt. Stir constantly to avoid burning the chocolate.
3. Once the chocolate is fully melted, about 3 to 4 minutes, and the ingredients are thoroughly incorporated, remove the pan from the heat.
4. Add the vanilla and (if desired) the nuts, and stir for 3 minutes.
5. Pour the fudge mixture into the baking dish, spreading it evenly.
6. Chill the fudge for 2 hours.
7. Cut the fudge into 30 squares and serve.

NOTES
If the fudge seems too stiff when pouring it into the pan, add 1 teaspoon of milk and stir completely.

Mince Pies

During the trio's third year, mince pies arrived via owl mail for the winter holidays. This compact, flaky Christmas dish is quite easy for owls to transport.

Yield
12 to 14 mincemeat pies

Prep time
1 hour, plus 1 hour to rest

Cook time
8 hours, plus 30 to 40 minutes

Mincemeat
2 pounds finely
chopped beefsteak
2 cups raisins
2 cups finely chopped
dried apricots
2 tart apples, finely chopped
1 cup vegetable shortening
2 cups brown sugar
peels of 2 limes, shredded
peels of 2 lemons, shredded
juice of 2 limes
juice of 2 lemons
2 tablespoons apple cider vinegar
2 tablespoons finely
chopped almonds
12 ounces peach nectar
1½ teaspoons ground cinnamon
½ teaspoon ground nutmeg
¼ teaspoon ground cloves
¼ teaspoon ground allspice
¼ teaspoon ground ginger
¼ teaspoon ground coriander
¼ teaspoon ground
mace (optional)
2 tablespoons brandy or
dark rum (optional)
Pastry Crust (page 109)

1. Combine all of the ingredients for the mincemeat in a slow cooker and cook on low for 8 hours.
2. Remove the mincemeat from the slow cooker once done and strain the ingredients, if any liquid remains. Set aside.
3. A couple of hours before you are ready to assemble the pie, make the Pastry Crust.
4. Once the mincemeat is ready and the Pastry Crust has risen, preheat the oven to 375°F.
5. Remove the dough from the refrigerator and punch it out to soften it into a moldable texture. If the dough is dry at all, add a tablespoon of ice water and work it into the dough until it is smooth and solid.
6. Place the dough on a floured surface and roll it out to a ¼- to ½-inch thickness.
7. Use a large-mouthed glass or biscuit cutter to cut out circles of dough.
8. Line a muffin tin with the dough circles.
9. Fill the dough cups about halfway with mincemeat.
10. Cut the remainder of the dough into strips or cut into decorative shapes.
11. Lay the strips or decorative shapes over the mince cups; lay strips in crosses or stripes.
12. Place the muffin tin in the oven and bake for 30 to 40 minutes, until the dough is lightly browned.
13. Remove from the oven and let cool for 5 minutes before serving hot.

Pastry Crust

2½ cups all-purpose flour

2 tablespoons granulated sugar

½ teaspoon salt

10 tablespoons cold butter, cut into chunks

6 tablespoons vegetable shortening, chilled and cut into chunks

8 to 12 tablespoons ice water

1. Add the flour, sugar, and salt to the bowl of a food processor. Pulse the dry ingredients a few times to combine.
2. Next, scatter the butter and shortening over the flour mixture, and pulse several times until the mixture resembles coarse meal. There should be no powdery residue left.
3. Transfer the mixture to a large mixing bowl.
4. Sprinkle 8 tablespoons of cold water over the mixture.
5. Use a spatula to toss the mixture together with the water until it begins to clump together.
6. If it's too dry, add more water in, 1 tablespoon at a time. It's better for it to be a little too wet than too dry.
7. Gather the dough into 2 equal balls and pat them into discs.
8. Wrap the discs in plastic wrap and refrigerate for 1 hour to rise.

Spring Recipes

With the winter thaw comes spring rain, new leaves, and fresh breezes. Though some might mourn the winter holidays and dread the approaching spring exams, there is still a lot to celebrate during springtime. Valentine's Day, Easter, and warmer, sunnier weather are all fast approaching. And with all of those things comes more delicious food!

Valentine's Day Tea

Valentine's Day is really what you make of it. For the (arguably) silliest dark arts teacher, it might mean heart-shaped confetti, bunches of pink flowers, and dwarves wearing Cupid costumes. For others it might mean a first date at the tea shop in the village, decorated for the holiday with pink confetti and a cherub theme. Who knows, you might get a Valentine note that compares the color of your eyes to the skin of a toad. How romantic!

Petit Four Cakes

The perfect treat for a Valentine-themed tea, these little cakes taste as pretty as they look. If you have a heart-shaped cookie cutter, use that to shape your petit fours. Decorate with flowers or pink icing; it's up to you!

Yield
30 to 36 cakes

Prep time
30 to 35 minutes

Chill time
2 hours

your choice of 9 x 13-inch cake, completely cooled, with firm bottom
your choice of filling(s)
1 (12-ounce) package candy melts

Icing (optional)
5 cups powdered sugar
4 tablespoons milk
1 tablespoon extract flavor (such as almond, lemon, orange, or peppermint) or fresh fruit juice of choice

Decorations
icing, decorative sprinkles, candies, or other garnishes

Filling Suggestions
jams or preserves with flavor profiles that match the cake
caramel syrup
buttercream frosting
chocolate syrup
whipped cream
custard or pudding

1. Cut the cake into rectangular sixths.
2. Cut each sixth into 2 layers and remove the top layer from the first section of cake.
3. On the bottom half of the section, layer on frosting, jam, or another filling choice in a medium-thin layer.
4. Place the top portion of the section on top of the coated cake.
5. Repeat with the other sections of the cake.
6. Next, cut each sixth of the cake into fourths.
7. Line your baking sheets with parchment paper and place the petit fours on the baking sheets, with an inch or two between each miniature cake.
8. If using candy melts, place the melts in a microwavable dish and melt in 30-second increments, stirring between each increment. When the candy melts are smooth and flowing from the spoon, they're ready to top the cakes. If using icing, combine all of the ingredients in a bowl and mix by hand until the icing is smooth and flowing.
9. Drizzle your candy melts or icing over each individual cake.
10. Decorate the cakes with either piped icing or decorative sprinkles, candies, or other garnish of choice.
11. Place in the refrigerator for 2 hours to solidify the frosting or candy coating.
12. If there's excess icing or candy coating, use a butter knife to trim the excess off after they've been chilled.

Heart-Shaped Sugar Cookies

This classic sugar cookie recipe goes well with tea or coffee. Even if you're on an awkward first date, you'll be able to enjoy some tasty cookies while picking pink confetti out of your teacup.

Yield
3 dozen cookies

Prep time
20 minutes

Cook time
7 to 9 minutes

Chill time
2 hours

3 cups all-purpose flour
¾ teaspoon baking powder
¼ teaspoon salt
1 cup unsalted butter, softened
1 cup cane sugar
1 egg, beaten
1 tablespoon milk
powdered sugar, for
rolling out dough

Icing
1 cup powdered sugar
2 teaspoons milk
2 teaspoons light corn syrup
¼ teaspoon vanilla or
almond extract
food coloring

1. In a medium bowl, sift together the flour, baking powder, and salt. Set aside.
2. Next, place the butter and sugar in a large mixing bowl. Beat with an electric handheld mixer on medium speed until the mixture turns light in color.
3. Add the egg and milk to the butter mixture and combine completely.
4. With the mixer on low speed, gradually add the flour mixture and beat until the mixture pulls away from the side of the bowl.
5. Divide the dough in half, wrap it in waxed paper, and refrigerate it for 2 hours.
6. Once the dough has chilled, preheat the oven to 375°F.
7. Sprinkle your rolling surface with powdered sugar. Sprinkle the rolling pin with powdered sugar, as well.
8. Remove one of the dough packs from the refrigerator.
9. Roll the dough out to approximately ¼-inch thickness. Make sure the dough isn't sticking.
10. If the dough winds up getting warm as you roll it out, place a cold cookie sheet over the rolled-out dough for 10 minutes to cool.
11. Use your heart-shaped cookie cutters to cut out the cookies. Place the cookie dough shapes 1 inch apart on a greased cookie sheet.
12. Place the cookie sheet in the oven, and bake the cookies for 7 to 9 minutes or until they are just beginning to brown around the edges.
13. While the first round of cookies is cooling, remove the second dough pack from the refrigerator and repeat the process of rolling out, cutting, and baking the cookies. Let them cool completely before frosting all the cookies.
14. Make the icing. In a small bowl, mix together the powdered sugar and milk until smooth. Beat in the corn syrup and extract, until the

icing is glossy and smooth. If the icing is too thick, add a little bit
more corn syrup. Divide the icing into the number of bowls of icing
colors you'd like to create. Add 1 or 2 drops of coloring to each
batch until the desired color is achieved.

15. Once the cookies are completely cooled, use a brush to paint the
icing onto the cookies.

Dainty Tea Sandwiches

Here are four different tea sandwiches that cater to almost everyone: vegetarians, picky eaters, and meat lovers alike. Feel free to tweak the ingredients.

<u>Yield</u>
3 sandwiches per 2 slices of bread

<u>Prep time</u>
2 to 3 minutes per sandwich

<u>Ham and Cheese</u>
soft wheat, honey wheat, or similar "light" flavored bread
sliced deli ham
sliced Swiss cheese or 1 large wedge of Brie
butter (omit with Brie)

<u>Cream Cheese and Cucumber</u>
soft wheat, honey wheat, or similar "light" flavored bread
1 medium cucumber
cream cheese, softened
handful of fresh cilantro leaves
dried oregano

<u>Smoked Salmon and Cream Cheese</u>
soft wheat, honey wheat, or similar "light" flavored bread
smoked salmon
cream cheese, softened

<u>Pepperoni and Cream Cheese</u>
soft wheat, honey wheat, or similar "light" flavored bread
pepperoni slices
cream cheese, softened
dash of thyme, rosemary, and/ or ground black pepper

1. For each sandwich, you will spread a thin to moderate layer of cream cheese or butter on one side of both slices of bread. For the ham and Brie, spread the Brie.
2. Layer on the meat, fish, or vegetable ingredients thickly. This is especially important for the pepperoni and the salmon.
3. Layer on any cheese toppings in a single-slice layer.
4. Add any additional ingredients in a thin layer on top of the ingredients or lightly sprinkle seasoning over the other ingredients.
5. Top with closing bread slice.
6. Cut off the crusts of the sandwiches and cut each into three sections.
7. Serve immediately for the freshest flavor.

Owl-Mail Feast

When your godfather is on the run from the authorities, it's important that he keep up his strength. The next set of recipes are inspired by the care package the trio sends via owl mail to help a certain marauder stay well fed in the village outside Hogwarts. The ham, a dozen buns, and the fruit in the care package no doubt lasted for several days, but also required several owls to carry the bounty.

Citrus-Glazed Ham

This recipe uses a precooked ham to make all non-magical lives a little easier. What really makes this ham shine is the deliciously sweet glaze that encourages the ham to remain tender and flavorful while it bakes in the oven. The juice left over in the pan after baking is exceptionally tasty and should be preserved until the ham is eaten. It can be reheated with the leftover ham and spooned over it to help keep everything moist.

Yield
1 serving per ¾ pound
(bone-in ham)

Prep time
15 minutes

Cook time
3 hours

Glaze
½ cup orange juice
½ cup pineapple juice
1½ cups packed light-brown sugar

Ham
1 precooked ham, bone-in
2 oranges, sliced
2 lemons, sliced

1. Preheat the oven to 350°F.
2. To make the glaze, add the orange juice, pineapple juice, and brown sugar to a medium saucepan. Stir the mixture over medium heat until the sugar dissolves.
3. Bring the glaze to a gentle boil, then remove it from the heat and set aside.
4. Thoroughly rinse the ham with cool water, then place it in a large baking pan.
5. Surround the ham with the orange and lemon slices, smearing the slices across the ham and lightly squeezing a little juice out.
6. Gently spoon the glaze over the top of the ham until the whole ham has been covered and the glaze is used up.
7. Cover the dish with aluminum foil and place it in the oven.
8. Bake for 1 hour, 30 minutes.
9. Pull the ham partially out of the oven and uncover it. Spoon the glaze and juices over the ham several times to moisten the meat.
10. Re-cover and bake again for another 1 hour, 30 minutes.
11. Remove from the oven and remove the foil. Let cool for 5 minutes before carving.

A Dozen Cakes (Sweet Buns)

Inspired by traditional Russian sweet buns called vatrushka, these are a little more substantial than other sweet breads, thanks to their cheesy filling. If a person was on the run from a magical governing body, it would certainly help to have these portable yet delicious buns on hand.

Yield
12 servings

Prep time
40 minutes

Wait time
1 hour

Cook time
20 minutes

4½ cups all-purpose flour, plus more for kneading and rolling

1 tablespoon fast-acting yeast

1 cup sugar

1 teaspoon salt

1 cup warm water

2 eggs, beaten, divided

4 tablespoons butter, softened

sesame seeds, for topping (optional)

Filling
12 teaspoons cream cheese, softened

12 teaspoons jam or preserves

1. In a medium mixing bowl, combine the flour, yeast, sugar, and salt. Mix until completely blended.
2. Add the water and half of the beaten eggs, blending them thoroughly into the dry mix.
3. Add the butter and mix until combined.
4. Remove the dough from the bowl and place it on a heavily floured surface. Knead the dough until it is smooth and elastic.
5. Place the dough back in the mixing bowl and cover. Keep the bowl in a warm place for 1 hour for the dough to rise.
6. Preheat the oven to 400°F.
7. Remove the cover from the mixing bowl. When the dough has risen, punch the dough down.
8. Roll the dough into a dozen balls of equal size.
9. Sprinkle flour on a surface and roll out each ball individually. They should be thick disks of about ½-inch thickness.
10. To make the filling, spread approximately 1 teaspoon of softened cream cheese onto the center of the dough piece.
11. Add a dollop of about 1 teaspoon of your choice of preserves or jam onto the cream cheese in the middle of the dough.
12. Pull up the sides of dough around the filling and pinch them together in the center to create a bun.
13. Repeat with all 12 balls of dough, placing each completed bun on a well-greased baking sheet.
14. Brush the remaining beaten egg onto the top of each of the buns. Top with sesame seeds, if using.
15. Bake for 20 minutes or until golden brown.
16. Let cool for 10 minutes and serve.

Fresh Fruit Salad

This recipe is for a delicious fruit salad, inspired by the whole fruit that was most likely in the care package. A perfect springtime side for any meal, you can customize this recipe to include all of your favorite fruit.

Yield
10 servings

Prep time
30 minutes

half a watermelon
2 apples
2 bananas
1 cantaloupe
1 pint strawberries
1 pint blueberries
1 pineapple
1 pound red or green grapes
whipped cream (optional)

1. Chop all the fruit—minus the blueberries and grapes—into bite-size pieces.
2. Mix all of the fruit together in a large serving bowl and chill for 2 hours.
3. Serve with dollops of whipped cream, if desired.

Easter

Easter is celebrated at Hogwarts with two weeks of holidays. Many students head home for those couple of weeks, while others decide to stay at the castle. The downside to the Easter holiday is the amount of schoolwork the professors often assign their classes. It certainly doesn't feel like a holiday if you're in the library with your friends working through piles of assignments! Luckily, a care package can brighten up those dreary days.

Toffee-Filled Easter Eggs

Chocolate Easter eggs filled with toffee—what a nice surprise to receive in the mail! That is, until you realize your eggs are only the size of a chicken's, while your two best friends have gotten eggs the size of a dragon's. Don't be too put out. Sometimes you can't help the gossip that's published in magazines, even if all of it is completely untrue. Here's a recipe that you can make at home. (And if you want to make a variety of different sizes and give the smallest one to the friend that you're mad at, that's totally up to you.)

Yield
12 to 16 eggs, depending on mold size

Prep time
25 minutes

Cook time
12 to 15 minutes

Cool time
1 to 2 hours

high-quality melting chocolate
Toffee Sauce Filling (page 129)
egg-shaped candy molds

1. Melt the chocolate in the microwave in 30-second increments, stirring between each round.
2. Once the chocolate is fully melted and smooth, remove it from the microwave and prepare the candy molds.
3. Lightly drizzle the chocolate into the 2 egg-shaped molds that are the same size.
4. Gently pat the chocolate into the edges to completely fill the molds.
5. Chill the chocolate for 1 hour.
6. Fill the chocolate shells in one of the molds with the Toffee Sauce Filling to make the first half of the eggs.
7. Place the second egg mold on top of the toffee-filled egg mold to complete the eggs. Gently remove the top mold.
8. Remelt the remaining chocolate.
9. Let the chocolate cool slightly so that it no longer drizzles.
10. Gently pat the soft chocolate along the edges of the eggs to seal in the toffee sauce.
11. Place the eggs back in the refrigerator and chill for another 1 to 2 hours, until the eggs are completely solid.
12. Remove the eggs gently from the mold and place on a lined baking sheet or bowl for serving.

Toffee Sauce Filling

1 cup granulated sugar
⅓ cup water
¾ cup heavy whipping cream
2 tablespoons unsalted butter
1 teaspoon vanilla extract

1. Add the sugar to a saucepan. Shake it out until it evenly covers the bottom of the pan.
2. Add the water to fully moisten the sugar.
3. Place the pot over medium heat and cook until the sugar dissolves and turns clear.
4. Raise the heat to medium-high. Cook the ingredients until they turn an amber color.
5. Turn the heat off and add the heavy whipping cream to the pan. The caramel may harden quickly and become difficult to work with.
6. Add the butter and stir until the sauce smooths out. If it's still lumpy, turn the heat back on to medium, and gently stir until it's smooth.
7. When it's finished cooking, add the vanilla extract.
8. Let the sauce cool to room temperature and then transfer it to a jar with a lid.
9. Chill the sauce until it is cold to the touch before making the eggs.

Classic Castle Breakfast

It's important for growing witches and wizards to have a wholesome first meal of the day. With busy days packed with difficult classes, starting the morning right will set you up for success.

Kippers

Kippers are butterflied and smoked herring that are usually eaten for breakfast, and are a frequent component of the first meal of the day at the castle. This recipe is for a sandwich, making kippers a little more palatable for those who aren't used to fish for breakfast!

Yield
2 servings

Prep time
5 minutes

Cook time
20 to 25 minutes

1 teaspoon salt
2 teaspoons white vinegar
4 cold eggs
2 herring fillets or 1 cup marinated herring in wine sauce
cream cheese
4 slices toast
garlic powder, to serve
rosemary, to serve
black pepper, to serve

1. Put 2 inches of water into a saucepan.
2. Add the salt and vinegar to the pan and bring them to a simmer over medium heat.
3. In a separate bowl, crack 2 cold eggs into 2 ramekins or custard cups.
4. Use the handle of your spatula or spoon to quickly stir the water in one direction, creating a whirlpool action in the water mixture.
5. Pour the 2 eggs into the center of the whirlpool. The swirling contains the eggs and prevents them from feathering out into the pan.
6. Turn off the heat, cover the pan, and set a timer for 5 minutes. Leave the eggs alone during this time.
7. Use a slotted spoon to remove the eggs and place them on a plate.
8. Repeat with the second batch of 2 eggs.
9. While the second batch of eggs is poaching, place the herring in a preheated cast-iron skillet and cook until both sides are browned. Add a hint of oil throughout if needed to keep the fish from sticking to the pan.
10. Remove the fish from the pan and serve them with cream cheese–smeared toast and poached eggs.
11. Sprinkle the garlic powder, rosemary, and black pepper over the eggs.

NOTES

If you don't like poached eggs, you can also just scramble together the bits of herring with the eggs, then serve them as a plate or as a sandwich combining all elements, including the cream cheese. Dipping the sandwich in ketchup is also great.

Eggs and Bacon

If kippers aren't quite your cup of tea, here's a recipe for eggs and bacon using traditional American bacon. You can cook the bacon either in an oven or in a skillet on the stovetop. Either way, be sure to save all of that flavorful bacon grease to cook your eggs. This is key!

Yield

2 servings

Cook time

20 to 40 minutes

8 strips bacon
4 to 6 eggs
celery seed
ground pepper
salt
garlic powder
minced onion

To Cook the Bacon in the Oven

1. Preheat the oven to 375°F.
2. Line a rimmed baking sheet with foil and lay out the bacon strips side by side. Cook the bacon for 15 to 20 minutes, then flip.
3. Cook the bacon on the other side for another 8 to 10 minutes or until it is crisp all the way through.
4. Set aside the bacon grease for cooking the eggs.

To Cook the Bacon on the Stovetop

1. Preheat a cast-iron skillet or stainless-steel skillet for 2 to 3 minutes over medium-low heat.
2. Place the bacon strips side by side in the pan.
3. Once the bacon begins to crisp some, about 3 minutes, flip the strips with tongs.
4. Cook on the other side until the bacon is crisped through, about 3 minutes.
5. Leave the bacon grease in the pan for cooking the eggs.

To Cook the Eggs

1. Once the bacon grease is in the preheated skillet, crack open the eggs into the pan.
2. Lightly sprinkle all of the spices over the tops of the eggs.
3. For sunny-side up, cook the eggs until they are solid and crisping around the edges, about 5 minutes.
4. If you prefer over-easy eggs, use a spatula to turn the eggs over and finish cooking until they are lightly brown on both sides, about 5 minutes each side.

Porridge

A breakfast staple around the world, there's almost nothing more comforting than a bowl of warm porridge in the morning. Whether you've got a difficult potion to make, a transfiguration spell to work on, or broomstick practice, porridge will fill you up and give you the energy you need to take on the day!

Yield
4 servings

Total time
10 to 12 minutes

2 cups rolled oats
2 cups 2% milk or whole milk
1 to 2 tablespoons of topping choice

Suggested Toppings
1 tablespoon maple syrup
1 tablespoon brown sugar
1 tablespoon jam
¾ tablespoon honey
handful of pecans or almonds
handful of dried fruit
sliced banana

1. Add the oats and milk to a medium saucepan. Stir them together until the oats are covered in milk.
2. Bring up the heat to medium and gently bring to a boil, stirring often.
3. Once the oats start to thicken, lower the heat to avoid burning.
4. Allow the oats to simmer for 5 to 7 minutes on low heat, stirring often.
5. Remove the oats from the heat and let them stand for 1 minute.
6. Dish out the porridge into serving vessels and stir in the toppings.

Summer Recipes

For our favorite dark wizard defeater, summer is not a happy season. He has to say goodbye to his closest friends and return to his terrible relatives' house. But for those of us who have fonder associations with the warmest season of the year, it's a time to enjoy the nice weather, the sunshine, and some wonderful group get-togethers. In this section you'll find classic recipes like burgers and cake pops, as well as fancier recipes for more important occasions.

Cousin's Birthday

The following recipes are sure to satisfy even the greediest of cousins. Burgers and a gloriously decadent ice cream sundae—what could be better?

Burgers

Burgers are arguably one of the best things to eat at a summer birthday party. Is there anything better than backyard grilling with friends and family? This healthier take on the classic burger is a guaranteed crowd-pleaser, even for the birthday boy who got *only* 36 presents!

<u>Yield</u>
4 burgers

<u>Prep time</u>
10 to 15 minutes

<u>Cook time</u>
10 to 20 minutes

1 pound ground turkey
½ teaspoon ground black pepper
1 teaspoon garlic powder
1 tablespoon oregano
½ tablespoon minced onion
½ teaspoon dried rosemary
4 buns
condiments of choice, like ketchup, mustard, or mayonnaise
toppings of choice, like lettuce, tomato, onion, and cheese

1. Preheat the grill or a cast-iron skillet over medium heat.
2. In a medium mixing bowl, combine the ground turkey and all of the seasonings. Use a fork to fully incorporate the seasonings into the meat.
3. Once the spices are thoroughly incorporated, use your hands to create four patties.
4. Place the patties on the cooking surface and cook for 5 to 10 minutes.
5. Flip the burger and cook again for 5 to 10 minutes, or until done.
6. While the burgers are cooking, add any condiments to your buns, as desired.
7. Remove the burgers from the cooking surface, place each patty on half of a bun, layer on the toppings, as desired, and top with the other half of a bun.
8. Serve immediately.

Knickerbocker Glory

The Knickerbocker Glory is an ice cream extravaganza. With layers of ice cream, fruit, nuts, sauce, and whatever else you'd like, this dessert is perfect for any birthday or special occasion. Try setting up a toppings station so all of your guests can concoct their own versions!

<u>Yield</u>
6 servings

<u>Prep time</u>
5 to 10 minutes

<u>Cook time</u>
10 minutes

1.5 quarts vanilla ice cream
1 (8-ounce) tub whipped cream
4 to 8 ounces frozen mixed berries
3 tablespoons peanuts, chopped (optional), to garnish

<u>Raspberry Sauce</u>
½ cup cane sugar
3 tablespoons water
12 ounces frozen raspberries

1. To make the raspberry sauce, combine the sugar and water in a medium saucepan over medium heat and stir them together until the sugar mostly dissolves.
2. Add the raspberries in small chunks. Wait for each chunk to soften slightly before adding the next chunk.
3. Bring the sauce to a gentle boil, stirring constantly, then remove from the heat and let cool for 2 minutes.
4. If you are using glass serving dishes, place a metal spoon in each serving vessel to dispel heat.
5. Add 2 tablespoons of the raspberry sauce to each glass.
6. Add 1 small scoop of vanilla ice cream to each glass.
7. Add 1 large dollop of whipped cream to each glass.
8. Add a handful of frozen berries to each glass.
9. Repeat layering with the sauce, ice cream, whipped cream, and berries, until each glass is full.
10. Top with the remaining raspberry sauce.
11. Garnish with chopped peanuts, if desired.

Uncle's Important Dinner Party

An important dinner party with your uncle's boss isn't the best time for a house elf to be marauding around your home. But when you're the protagonist, these things tend to happen. And hey, even if the dessert ends up on someone's head and the punchline of a golf joke gets ruined, at least the magical creature had your best interests at heart!

Roast Pork

When trying to impress a boss—whether someone else's or your own—it's best to stick with a tried-and-true classic. This roast pork recipe is sure to impress even the most crotchety of employers, thanks to a flavor-packed spice rub and a beautiful glaze.

Yield
8 servings

Prep time
15 minutes

Cook time
1 to 1½ hours

Rest time
10 minutes

3 pounds pork loin
1 tablespoon olive oil
whole cloves (optional)

Spice Rub
1 teaspoon paprika
1 teaspoon garlic powder
½ teaspoon onion powder
½ teaspoon dried thyme
½ teaspoon dried rosemary
¼ teaspoon salt
½ teaspoon freshly ground black pepper

Glaze
4 cloves garlic, minced
¼ cup honey
1 cup applesauce
1 tablespoon olive oil
1 can whole-berry cranberry sauce

1. Make the spice rub by combining all of the spices together in a bowl. Set aside.
2. Make the glaze by combining all of the ingredients, save the cranberry sauce, in a bowl. Set aside, reserving the cranberry sauce for the last 30 minutes of cooking.
3. Preheat the oven to 375°F.
4. Line a metal pan with aluminum foil or use an ungreased glass baking pan. Set aside.
5. Thoroughly rinse the pork loin and pat it dry with paper towels. Lightly spray the pork loin with cooking spray.
6. Rub the spice rub all over the pork, on all sides, save the fatty side.
7. Pour the oil into a skillet and bring it to medium heat.
8. Once the oil is heated, place the pork in the oiled pan and gently sear the pork on all sides.
9. Transfer the pork to the metal pan lined with aluminum foil or the ungreased glass baking pan, with the fatty layer–side up.
10. Brush the glaze over the pork and leave the remainder of the sauce in the pan with the pork, reserving 2 tablespoons.
11. Garnish the meat with the whole cloves, if using.
12. Roast for 25 minutes.
13. Pull the oven rack out and baste the pork with the sauce in the pan.
14. Return the pork to the oven and roast for another 25 minutes.
15. Pull the oven rack out once more, and use the reserved cranberry sauce and glaze to cover the pork roast again.
16. Return the pork to the oven and roast it for 10 to 15 minutes, or until the internal temperature of the pork reaches 145°F on a meat thermometer.
17. Remove the pork from the oven and let it stand for 10 minutes before slicing.
18. Serve with whatever garnishes you prefer, like sliced citrus, parsley, or a side of potatoes.

Sugared Violet Cake

Is there anything more fussy than sugared violets? Actually yes, and it's called a Spanische Windtorte. No, we didn't just sneeze, that's the name of the pudding that a certain fussy aunt served at her husband's important dinner party. This historical dessert is complex and difficult to make, so we've taken mercy on you, dear reader. We've used the Spanische Windtorte as the inspiration for an easy-to-make, delicious cake. The recipe below still features plenty of sugared violets and whipped cream, so it'll still make a massive impact when magically dumped on someone's head!

Yield
12 servings

Prep time
20 minutes

Cook time
35 minutes

1¼ cups powdered sugar

¾ cup plus 2 tablespoons all-purpose flour

1½ cups egg whites, room temperature (approximately 11 to 12 egg whites)

1½ teaspoons cream of tartar

1½ teaspoons vanilla extract

¼ teaspoon almond extract (optional)

¼ teaspoon salt

1 cup granulated sugar

1 (8-ounce) tub whipped cream

sugared violets

1. Preheat the oven to 375°F.
2. In a medium bowl, whisk together the powdered sugar and flour. Set aside.
3. With an electric handheld mixer or stand mixer, combine the egg whites, cream of tartar, vanilla extract, almond extract (if desired), and salt. Mix together well.
4. With the mixer on high, beat in the sugar, 1 tablespoon at a time. Add each tablespoon only once the previous spoonful has been dissolved. Do not scrape the sides of the bowl as you do this, just keep beating.
5. Now, beat this mixture until stiff peaks form. The mixture will be thick, glossy, and sticky.
6. Using a rubber spatula, gently fold the sugar and flour mixture into the egg mixture, ½ cup at a time. Don't overmix.
7. Keep folding the sugar and flour mixture in until the flour mixture is completely combined into the egg mixture.
8. Pour everything into an ungreased 9-inch round pan or 10-inch tube pan.
9. Use a knife or spatula to cut through the batter to break up any bubbles.

10. Bake the cake for 35 minutes, or until the top of the cake springs back when lightly touched. Cracks on the surface should look dry.
11. Remove the cake from the oven and immediately invert on a cooling rack or bottle, if using a tube pan.
12. Allow the cake to cool completely before placing it right-side up.
13. Cover the cake with whipped cream from the tub.
14. Decorate it with sugared violets and serve.

NOTES

You can purchase sugared violets from multiple outlets, if you don't have the time or inclination to make them yourself. Fresh violets can be used instead of sugared, if preferred.

A July 31st Birthday

When July comes around it's time to celebrate
the birthday of our favorite bespectacled
main character. From a bedroom under the
stairs to (spoiler alert!) marriage and kids,
we've shared countless experiences with this
wonderful boy, so it's only right to celebrate
his birthday with a delicious treat. In honor
of the birthday boy's favorite sport, here
is a fun recipe for golden cake pops.

Golden Birthday Cake Pops

This cake pop recipe is punchier than a normal vanilla cake, thanks to some added lemon juice and lemon zest. The bright, citrusy flavor is inspired by the zippiness of the enchanted golden ball, but feel free to adjust the citrus measurements to your own taste!

Yield

24 to 30 cake pops

Prep time

1 to 1½ hours

Chill time

1½ hours

Cook time

25 to 30 minutes

Cake

3 cups all-purpose flour

¼ teaspoon baking soda

2¾ teaspoons baking powder

1 teaspoon salt

1½ cups unsalted butter, room temperature

2 cups cane sugar

4 egg whites

1½ teaspoons vanilla extract

1¼ cups milk

¼ cup fresh lemon juice

2 tablespoons lemon zest

yellow candy melts

lollipop or cake pop sticks

fondant sheets

To Make the Cake

1. Preheat the oven to 350°F.
2. Grease the bottom and sides of a 9 x 12-inch cake pan with cooking spray.
3. Combine the flour, baking soda, baking powder, and salt in a medium bowl. Set aside.
4. Add the butter and sugar to a large mixing bowl, and beat with an electric handheld mixer on medium speed until fluffy and light.
5. Add the egg whites and vanilla extract, and mix thoroughly until well combined. Scrape down the sides.
6. Add in one third of the flour mixture to the creamy mixture, and beat on medium speed until fully incorporated.
7. Next, add one half of the milk, lemon juice, and lemon zest. Beat on medium speed until thoroughly incorporated.
8. Repeat steps 6 and 7 until all of the ingredients have been thoroughly combined.
9. Pour the batter into the cake pan and bake for 25 to 30 minutes or until a toothpick comes out clean from the middle of the cake.
10. Remove the cake from the oven and allow it to cool for 2 minutes.
11. Remove the cake from the pan and put it on a cooling rack.
12. Let cool completely before making the cake pops.

Icing

¼ cup unsalted butter,
room temperature
1½ cups powdered sugar
1 teaspoon lime juice
2½ teaspoons lemon juice
2½ teaspoons heavy
whipping cream

To Make the Icing

1. Combine all ingredients, save the whipping cream, in a medium mixing bowl and beat together until thoroughly incorporated.
2. Add the heavy whipping cream and beat again until light and fluffy. Set aside.

To Make the Cake Pops

1. To assemble the cake pops, break off one third of the cake and crumble it into a medium mixing bowl.
2. Add 2 tablespoons icing and mix with your hands or with an electric handheld mixer until the cake and frosting blend thoroughly.
3. If the cake and icing mixture isn't moist enough, add 1 tablespoon of icing at a time until you can shape the mixture into balls that are about the size of a quarter in diameter and that hold together without being gooey.
4. In a microwave-safe dish, warm the candy melts in a microwave oven until they're smooth and runny.
5. Line a baking sheet with parchment paper.
6. Take the lollipop sticks and dip one end into the melted candy. Stick the candy-dipped ends into the cake balls.
7. Chill the cake balls for 30 minutes in the refrigerator.
8. Once the cake balls have chilled, remove them from the refrigerator and reheat the candy if it has hardened.
9. Now, take the cake balls on the sticks and dip each one into the candy coating.
10. Place the cake pops on a lined baking sheet and let them chill for 1 hour.
11. Once the cake pops have solidified, use a knife to gently trim any excess candy coating.
12. Cut the fondant sheets into feather shapes for the wings, making sure there are sharp points on one end for inserting into the cake pops.
13. Insert 2 of the fondant feathers on opposite sides of each cake pop.
14. Serve and enjoy.

A World Cup Dinner

The World Cup for the wizarding world's favorite sport is held every four years in different places around the globe, so it's always a big deal when it comes back to Britain. During their fourth year, our favorite trio is treated to a delicious al fresco dinner the night before the Cup. A warm meat pie paired with a light summer salad followed by a tart-but-sweet strawberry ice cream is the perfect meal to eat before the biggest sporting event in the wizardly world.

Creamy Chicken and Ham Pie

Thanks to a magic wand, it's certainly possible to whip up a perfectly baked meat pie with béchamel sauce while haranguing a certain set of twins about their latest mischievous endeavors. Unfortunately for those without wands, a kitchen with an oven and a stove is necessary. Feel free to enjoy this meal out in the garden like the trio did, but keep in mind it's best served warm.

Yield
8 servings

Prep time
40 to 50 minutes

Cook time
40 to 50 minutes

Wait time
1 hour

Pastry Crust (page 156)
4 tablespoons unsalted butter
4 green onions, chopped
½ cup all-purpose flour
1 cup chicken stock
1 cup fresh cilantro
2 stalks celery, chopped
4 cloves garlic, minced
1 cup cubed precooked ham
1 cup cubed precooked chicken
½ cup heavy cream
½ teaspoon sea salt
½ teaspoon ground pepper
4 egg yolks for egg wash
Béchamel (page 157)

1. Make the Pastry Crust.
2. Preheat the oven to 400°F.
3. Put the butter in a medium saucepan over medium heat.
4. Toss in the onions and stir for 2 minutes until the onions are warm and completely coated in the butter.
5. Reduce the heat and add the flour. Stir for 1 to 2 minutes.
6. Add the chicken stock and blend thoroughly.
7. Add the celery and minced garlic, and stir until the vegetables are coated.
8. Add the ham and chicken, and continuously stirring for 1 to 2 minutes.
9. Add the cream slowly, continuously stirring.
10. Finally, add, the salt and pepper.
11. Remove from the heat and let stand for 1 to 2 minutes before spooning the filling into the pie crust.
12. Take the remaining crust dough and position it around the top, pinching the edges together to seal the filling in and cover the pie fully.
13. Poke holes in the top crust to allow for proper ventilation.
14. Brush beaten egg yolks over the top of the crust.
15. Place the pie in the oven and bake it for 40 to 50 minutes, until the edges turn golden brown.
16. Remove the pie from the oven and let it stand while you make the Béchamel.
17. Spoon the Béchamel. over individual servings of pie and serve.

Pastry Crust

Yield
2 (9-inch) crusts

Prep time
25 to 30 minutes

Cool time
1 hour

2½ cups all-purpose flour
2 tablespoons granulated sugar
½ teaspoon salt
10 tablespoons cold butter, cut into chunks
6 tablespoons vegetable shortening, chilled and cut into chunks
8 to 12 tablespoons ice water

1. Add the flour, sugar, and salt to the bowl of a food processor.
2. Pulse the dry ingredients a few times to combine.
3. Scatter the butter and shortening over the flour mixture, and pulse several times until the mixture resembles coarse meal. There should be no powdery residue left.
4. Transfer the mixture to a large mixing bowl.
5. Sprinkle 8 tablespoons of cold water over the mixture.
6. Use a spatula to toss the mixture together with the water until it begins to clump together.
7. If it's too dry, add more water, 1 tablespoon at a time. It's better for it to be a little too wet than too dry.
8. Gather the dough into 2 equal balls and pat them into discs.
9. Wrap the discs in plastic wrap and refrigerate for 1 hour.
10. After the dough has chilled, remove it from the refrigerator and punch out the dough to soften it into a moldable texture. If the dough is sticky, add a tablespoon of flour. If it is dry, add a tablespoon of ice water.
11. Place 1 dough disc on a floured surface. Start in the middle of the disc and roll out into a large enough disc to line the bottom and sides of your pie pan. If you prefer, you can break the dough into smaller balls and put them around the pie tin and press out by hand.
12. Break the second ball into multiple small balls of dough, and roll out the dough or knead it out by hand if you prefer a thicker top crust. Set aside.

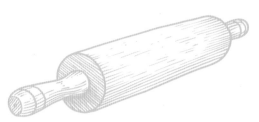

Béchamel

Prep time
2 to 3 minutes

Cook time
11 to 13 minutes

2 tablespoons butter
2 tablespoons all-purpose flour
1¼ cups milk, heated
salt
ground pepper
½ cup Parmesan cheese

1. Put the butter in a medium saucepan over medium heat.
2. Once the butter melts, add the flour and stir. The mixture will make a thick paste.
3. Keep stirring the paste until it thins out and begins to bubble. Do not let it brown.
4. Add the hot milk, continuing to stir.
5. Bring the sauce to a boil.
6. Add salt and pepper to taste.
7. Add Parmesan cheese, stirring until it is thoroughly incorporated.
8. Lower the heat and cook for 2 to 3 more minutes while continuously stirring.
9. Remove the sauce from the heat and let it cool for 1 to 2 minutes.

Summer Salad

This salad recipe features the bright sweetness of summer-fresh berries, which are always best during the warmer months. Paired with a flavorful dressing and some nuts for crunch, this side salad might become the hit of your summer party! Feel free to double the recipe, especially if you're cooking dinner for 11 people (many of whom are hungry teenagers).

<u>Yield</u>
4 to 6 servings

<u>Prep time</u>
10 to 15 minutes

<u>Chill time (dressing)</u>
1 to 2 hours

<u>Cilantro Honey Lime Dressing</u>
juice of 4 limes
½ cup orange blossom
or wildflower honey
4 teaspoons olive oil
4 teaspoons balsamic vinegar
½ cup packed fresh
cilantro, chopped

<u>Salad</u>
4 cups fresh, raw spinach
2 cups arugula
1 cup fresh raspberries
1 cup fresh blueberries
1 small white or red
onion, chopped
2 cups quinoa (cooked)
½ cup chopped almonds
¼ cup pine nuts
½ cup feta or bleu cheese
cilantro honey lime dressing

1. If possible, make the dressing 1 to 2 hours before using. Place all of the dressing ingredients in a jar or bottle with a water-tight lid. Vigorously shake the ingredients together until they are blended. Chill for 1 to 2 hours. Shake the dressing thoroughly before serving.
2. Toss the spinach and arugula in a large bowl.
3. Layer in each of the remaining ingredients, save the feta or bleu cheese, mixing the salad together well.
4. Top with cheese and cilantro honey lime dressing and serve.

Strawberry Ice Cream

Ice cream is the perfect dessert to finish off a summer dinner at your best friend's home. This recipe is easy to nail, and once you get the hang of it, you can experiment with different flavors for future batches.

Yield
12 servings

Prep time
15 minutes

Chill time
7 hours

1 pound frozen strawberries, thawed
2 cups cold heavy whipping cream
1 (14-ounce) can sweetened condensed milk
1 teaspoon vanilla extract

1. Before starting, place a freezer-safe loaf pan in the freezer for 1 hour.
2. After the pan has chilled, pulse the strawberries in a food processor until they are pulped into a thick, spreadable texture.
3. In a separate bowl, whip the heavy whipping cream with an electric handheld mixer on medium-high speed until firm peaks form.
4. Pour the pulped strawberries into a larger mixing bowl.
5. Fold about 1 cup of the whipped cream at a time into the strawberry mixture, until well blended.
6. Repeat until all of the whipped cream has been incorporated into the strawberry mixture.
7. Add the sweetened condensed milk and vanilla to the mixture, and blend thoroughly until smooth.
8. Pour the cream and strawberry mixture into the chilled pan and cover.
9. Freeze for 6 hours.
10. Remove from the freezer and serve.

Drinks for Any Season

At any holiday feast, drinks are nearly as important as the dishes being served. For both those of age and those under, here is a selection of magically delicious drinks that can be enjoyed with any of the feasts and dishes mentioned earlier in the cookbook. Cheers!

Butterscotch "Beer"

A wizarding world favorite, this "beer" recipe gives you both a hot and a cold option so that you can enjoy a cup full of butterscotch goodness all year round. It's the perfect beverage to sip while having a chat with your best friends, or while celebrating a big tournament win.

Yield

5 to 6 servings

Prep time

5 to 10 minutes

Cook time

5 to 7 minutes

1 cup butter

1½ cups butterscotch chips, plus extra for garnish

2 tablespoons light-brown sugar

3 tablespoons maple syrup

3 to 4 cups buttermilk (depending on hot or cold version)

whipped cream

2 cups ice, for cold version

chilled glasses, for cold version

Hot Version

1. In a medium saucepan over medium-low heat, melt the butter and butterscotch together until completely melted and smooth.
2. Add the brown sugar and maple syrup, and stir until melted and blended in thoroughly.
3. Next, pour in 4 cups of buttermilk. Keep mixing and stirring until the buttermilk comes to temperature.
4. Serve in a heat-resistant mug.
5. Top with whipped cream and garnish with additional butterscotch chips.

Cold Version

1. In a medium saucepan over medium-low heat, melt the butter and butterscotch together until completely melted and smooth.
2. Add the brown sugar and maple syrup, and stir until melted and blended in thoroughly.
3. Place the heated mixture in a blender.
4. Add 3 cups of buttermilk and the ice. Blend until smooth.
5. Pour into chilled glasses.
6. Top with whipped cream and garnish with additional butterscotch chips.

Pumpkin Juice

A beloved classic, pumpkin juice is served with nearly every meal at the castle, as well as on the scarlet steam engine. This recipe is best served well chilled and over ice.

<u>Yield</u>
6 servings

<u>Prep time</u>
5 minutes

<u>Chill time</u>
1 hour to overnight

2 cups apple cider or apple juice
1½ cups peach nectar
¾ cup pumpkin puree
¼ teaspoon ground cinnamon
¼ teaspoon ground nutmeg
¼ teaspoon pumpkin pie
spice or apple pie spice
2 teaspoons vanilla extract

1. In a large glass jar with a water-tight lid, combine all of the ingredients together.
2. Shake vigorously for 2 minutes or until everything is thoroughly combined.
3. Chill overnight for the richest pumpkin flavor. Shake thoroughly before serving over ice.

Fiery Whiskey

This recipe for a spicy whiskey shot is sure to have you and your friends feeling the burn, thanks to the hit of Tabasco. It takes several days to infuse the cinnamon flavor into the whiskey, so be sure to plan ahead.

<u>Yield</u>
1 shot

<u>Prep time</u>
5 minutes

<u>Age time</u>
4 to 7 days

30 milliliters whiskey
(about 1 shot)
2 cinnamon sticks
2 tablespoons brown sugar
1 teaspoon Tabasco sauce

1. Combine the whiskey, cinnamon, and brown sugar in a closed container.
2. Age the mixture for 4 to 7 days in a dark, cool place.
3. When ready to serve, add in ¼ teaspoon of Tabasco sauce per shot and let stand for 2 minutes before drinking.

Liquid Luck

Need all the help you can get before your big game? We feel you. This cocktail is full of flavor—and enough alcohol to have you feeling like the luckiest person in the room after emptying your glass. Be careful with this one. Like the potion it's inspired by, excessive consumption of this fortuitous cocktail can cause recklessness, giddiness, and other sorts of foolish behavior!

Yield

1 serving

Prep time

2 minutes

2 ounces bourbon
½ ounce orgeat syrup
½ teaspoon cardamom
drizzle of maple syrup
½ ounce lemon juice
½ ounce orange curaçao
orange peel and orange slice, for garnish

1. Toss everything except for the orange peel and slice into a shaker with ice.
2. Shake vigorously for 30 seconds.
3. Pour or strain into a small glass of your choosing.
4. Ring the rim with the orange peel and garnish with an orange slice, as desired.

Gill-Growing Weed Water

This refreshing drink won't help you grow gills and breathe underwater, but it is inspired by the mystic plant that does.

<u>Yield</u>
1 serving

<u>Prep time</u>
5 to 10 minutes

8 ounces sparkling
mineral water, chilled
½ teaspoon honey
juice of ½ lime
skin of ½ small cucumber
2 slices lemon
3 to 4 ice cubes

1. Juice the lime, skin the cucumber, and slice the lemon before pouring the mineral water.
2. Once the fresh ingredients are prepared, pour the mineral water and honey into a large glass and stir together immediately.
3. Add the fresh ingredients and the ice and stir once again.
4. Serve immediately to retain the fizz and sparkle.

Cherry Soda Drink

This recipe is inspired by the Charms professor's favorite drink. For an authentic and festive finish, add an umbrella.

<u>Yield</u>
1 serving

<u>Prep time</u>
3 minutes

8 ounces sparkling mineral water or seltzer water
¼ cup cherry pie filling
1 teaspoon cane sugar
dollop of whipped topping (optional)

1. In a 16- to 20-ounce glass, pour in the sparkling water.
2. Add the cherry pie filling and stir thoroughly.
3. Add the sugar and stir again.
4. If desired, top with a dollop of whipped cream.

Soul Sucker

This spiced coffee drink packs a punch—especially if you decide to spike it (we'd recommend Kahlúa, Irish cream, vodka, or any combination of these). Just make sure that your soul doesn't leave your body after your last sip!

Yield
2 servings

Prep time
10 minutes

Cook time
4 to 5 minutes

Wait time
10 minutes

Chill time
Overnight

Spiced Syrup
2 cups water
⅔ to 1 cup cane sugar, sweetened to taste
2 cinnamon sticks
2 teaspoons vanilla extract
2 teaspoons anise seeds
1 teaspoon nutmeg

Soul Sucker
2 cups medium roast coffee OR 2 cups dark black tea, such as Turkish Rize
2 cups chocolate milk
1 cup spiced syrup

1. Make the spiced syrup. Combine all of the ingredients in a saucepan and cook over medium-high heat. Constantly stirring, bring the ingredients to a gentle boil, dissolving the sugar completely. Remove from the heat and set aside to cool for 10 minutes before straining out the spices.
2. While the spiced syrup is cooling, combine the coffee or tea with the chocolate milk in a jar or shaker bottle with a water-tight lid.
3. Once the syrup is strained, combine 1 cup per 2 servings in the jar with the chocolate milk mixture.
4. Shake thoroughly until all ingredients are well combined.
5. Put the cocktail in the refrigerator. Chill overnight (approximately 8 hours) before serving.

Ice Potion

Beat the heat (whether it's from a magical fire protecting a very important stone, or otherwise) with this refreshingly cool watermelon beverage. Though it won't help you literally walk through a wall of fire, it's sure to help you cool down on a hot day.

Yield
6 servings

Prep time
15 minutes

Cook time
7 to 9 minutes

Chill time
1 hour

Strawberry Syrup
½ cup cane sugar
3 tablespoons water
12 ounces frozen strawberries

Ice Potion
6 cups seedless
watermelon, chopped
2 cups water
strawberry syrup
ice
fresh strawberry slices,
watermelon wedges, or
mint sprigs, to garnish

1. To make the strawberry syrup, combine the sugar and water in a medium saucepan over medium heat. Stir the sugar and water together until the sugar dissolves. Add chunks of the frozen strawberries (2 to 4 strawberries at a time). Stir until each chunk melts, then add the next chunk and repeat until all of the strawberries have been added. Bring to a gentle boil, stirring constantly. Remove from the heat and let cool completely before making the potion.
2. In a blender, blend the watermelon to a thick mixture that flows.
3. Pour the watermelon mixture into a large pitcher and add the water and strawberry syrup.
4. Fill serving glasses with ice and pour over ice.
5. Garnish with a fresh strawberry slice, watermelon wedge, or sprig of mint and serve.

Hot Chocolate

There's nothing more comforting than curling up with a cup of rich hot chocolate during a cold winter day. Try adding a variety of toppings to make your mug even more magical.

<u>Yield</u>
5 cups

<u>Total time</u>
12 to 15 minutes

½ cup cane sugar
¼ cup baking cocoa powder
dash of salt
⅓ cup hot water
4 cups milk
1 teaspoon extract (vanilla, peppermint, or almond)
miniature marshmallows, whipped cream, cinnamon sticks, or candy canes for garnish

1. In a saucepan, combine the sugar, cocoa powder, salt, and water. Stir together over medium-low heat and bring to a boil.
2. Cook for another 2 minutes, then stir in the milk.
3. Bring the mixture to serving temperature, but not boiling.
4. Remove from the heat and stir in the extract.
5. Whisk until frothy and pour into serving glasses or mugs.
6. Garnish, if desired, with miniature marshmallows, whipped cream, a cinnamon stick, or a candy cane (optional).

Fizzy Orange Juice

Inspired by our favorite fireworks-wielding twins, this sparkling soda drink tastes like an orange Creamsicle—but better.

<u>Yield</u>
10 servings

<u>Prep time</u>
10 minutes

orange juice
ground cinnamon
granulated sugar
2 liters orange soda, divided
2 cups cream soda
1 tablespoon vanilla extract
whipped cream
orange slices, orange peel, or vanilla beans, to garnish

1. Put the orange juice into a bowl large enough for the mouth of your glasses.
2. In a second bowl, large enough for the mouth of your glasses, combine the cinnamon and sugar.
3. Dip the mouth of each glass, one at a time, into the orange juice, followed by the cinnamon-and-sugar blend. Set the glasses aside.
4. Next, in a pitcher or bottle, put the orange soda, save 2 cups, along with the cream soda and vanilla. Stir or shake vigorously.
5. Mix in a few tablespoons of whipped cream, to taste, and stir or shake again.
6. Next, pour in the remaining 2 cups of orange soda to reengage the fizz.
7. Carefully pour the fizzy juice into the rimmed glasses, and garnish each drink with an orange slice, orange peel, or vanilla beans. Top with additional whipped cream if desired.

Polypotion Cocktail

After a couple of sips, this flavor-packed cocktail will have you feeling like a totally different person! This recipe is designed to look like what comes out of a bubbling cauldron, but is guaranteed to taste much more pleasant than what our trio tasted during their second year.

<u>Yield</u>
1 serving

<u>Prep time</u>
5 minutes

2 ounces vodka
1 scoop lime sherbet or sorbet
2 ounces lemon-lime soda
2 to 3 dashes bitters
1 teaspoon grenadine
or 2 teaspoons coconut milk (optional)
dried citrus slices and sprigs of mint (optional), to garnish

1. Pour the vodka into a large coupe glass. Add the sherbet.
2. Next, pour the lemon-lime soda over the sherbet in the glass.
3. Add the bitters to taste.
4. If using, add the grenadine, poured over the back of a spoon, or, instead of grenadine, add coconut milk and mix it in thoroughly.
5. Before serving, garnish with the decorations of your choice, if desired, like a slice of dried citrus or a sprig of mint.

Conclusion

Well, friends, here is where our journey together comes to an end. We hope you enjoyed the recipes in this cookbook, and we hope that they made your seasonal get-togethers and holidays a little bit more magical. As our favorite author once said, "Hogwarts will always be there to welcome you home," and we hope that this cookbook makes coming home for the holidays that much easier.

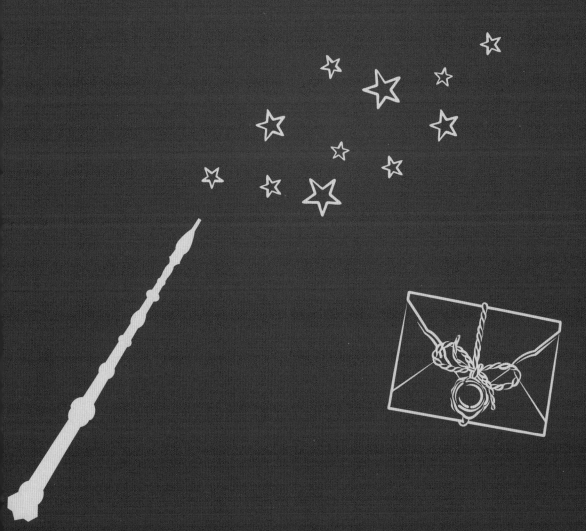

Acknowledgments

Special thanks to Justin Haferman for creating the amazing Liquid Luck and Andrew C. Anderson for the Butterscotch "Beer" and for connecting me with Justin. Shout-out to Cyndi Lublink for turning her kitchen into another testing kitchen for these amazing goodies (and her mom for the amazing Carrot Cake recipe!). Thanks to Helen Lee and the Galentine's ladies (and guys!)—including Julia Winter, Lisa Franklin, Marla Barch, Clarissa Simon, and Neal Simon—who helped me figure out portions for the Polypotion Cocktail and Fiery Whiskey. Thanks to David and Kitty Hobgood and Chris Hagberg for their love and support. Thanks, Sarah Bowler, Katrina Whaley, Bee George, Adam Estes, Nancy Richardson, and Christy Gallinger for the input on which recipes to develop and include in this delicious collection.

Finally, special thanks to my brother, Jeff Kirby, my mom, Nancy Mock, and my amazing hubby, Matt, for being such willing guinea pigs for the many, many recipes they noshed on and gave input for over the months of recipe development.

About the Author

Rita Mock-Pike is a freelance novelist, writer, and journalist. She has published works across multiple industries, both as a ghostwriter and as a bylined author. Thanks to living with her gourmet grandmother, Jerrie Mock (who also happens to be the first woman to fly around the world), home economics teacher mother, Nancy Mock, and cooking enthusiast father, Roger Mock, Rita has been cooking and creating recipes since she was seven years old. It was then that she began teaching her friends' moms how to cook something other than macaroni and cheese from a box. She hasn't stopped since, much to her husband's delight. She lives in Palatine, Illinois.